Marian Martin

The European Waterways
A User's Guide

SHERIDAN HOUSE

This edition published 2003 by
Sheridan House Inc.
145 Palisade Street
Dobbs Ferry, NY 10522
www.sheridanhouse.com

First edition 1997
Second edition 2003

Library of Congress Cataloging-in-Publication Data.

Martin, Marian.
  European waterways / Marian Martin.– 2nd ed.
    p. cm.
  ISBN 1-57409-176-X (alk. paper)
  1. Boats and boating–Europe–Guidebooks. 2.
Waterways–Europe–Guidebooks. I. Title.
GV776.42.A2 M37 2003
797.1'094–dc21

                    2003010281

Printed in Great Britian

ISBN 1-57409-176-X

Contents

Preface

Since the first edition of *European Waterways* was published, interest in inland waterway cruising has grown in leaps and bounds.

In the UK the first new waterways in centuries have recently been built, or are at the planning stage. In France, inland *ports de plaisance* have proliferated and existing ones have grown to accommodate increased demand, and every year more and more north Europeans and Scandinavians are to be found in southern France. Continental boat hire companies have built more bases, increased the number of boats in existing ones and expanded into Germany and Italy, as ever growing numbers decide to try this type of holiday.

Our enthusiasm for inland waterway wandering began many years ago, when friends invited us aboard their river cruiser. In those days, suggestions about where to go and factual information about what you needed to know when you got there was not easy to acquire. Even today, misleading information abounds. This book aims to dispel myths and provide the guidance you need to enjoy every aspect of inland waterway exploration, whether you are a complete newcomer to boating, or an old hand looking to expand your cruising horizons.

Sections on choice of boat, cruising grounds and waterway rules and regulations apply to all, but there are a number of subjects on which non-Europeans need specific information, so we have included a new chapter on this in the second edition.

We have also, at the request of many sailors, included a chapter with specific advice for those who do not want to linger inland, but need specific help in choosing and negotiating a through route to the Mediterranean.

So, wherever you set out from, this book will help you to find that ideal waterway and reach it without trauma. Read it before you set out, then keep it handy on board so that, unlike us and many other newcomers to inland waterways, you won't have to learn by your mistakes.

As in the previous edition, all handling techniques described in this book are based on the assumption that any boat will have a crew of at least two, because one person cannot safely manoeuvre a boat in all circumstances. In the case of narrow boats, we have assumed that any vessel over 50 feet (15 metres) long will have a minimum crew of three. From time to time one reads descriptions of gymnastic techniques invented by singlehanded cruisers to negotiate a particular lock or bridge. It is obvious that these acrobats are inordinately proud of their achievements but, in truth, many of the techniques are foolhardy, even dangerous.

The only real problem in writing this book has been deciding what to leave out. After a lot of discussion, we decided not to include information about basic boat handling, boating terminology, knot tying and various other bits of knowledge that are a precursor to happy cruising. Our logic was that these things have already been the subject of innumerable books and magazine articles, so our space could be better used to write about less well-documented subjects. In any case, we believe that anyone who takes up boating should take a course of instruction and obtain an appropriate qualification, and thus be familiar with things like current effect and clove hitches.

We also decided to minimise our use of boating parlance, for two reasons. Firstly, for example, saying anything other than 'Where's the loo/toilet/WC?' on an inland waterway cruiser is as inappropriate as taking a day trip to France and asking the ferry purser to direct you to 'the heads'! Secondly, you will want to invite friends on board and they may not be boating oriented so, in the interest of clear communication, it is much better to give instructions in everyday language.

There is, however, one 'foreign' expression that we have used throughout the book, because it is a lot simpler to adopt the French word *plaisancier* than to constantly write 'a person who is using a boat for pleasure purposes'. So read on, *plaisancier*, then go out and discover the ever-changing horizons that inland cruising will reveal to you.

Marian Martin

Why cruise inland?

'**W**here the voyage is more important than the destination' is the Gota Canal Steamship company's slogan, and nothing describes quite so aptly the principal reason that every boating enthusiast should try inland cruising. Once you start, you'll find that it is decidedly addictive. Every river bend brings a new view, every few miles along a canal there is another village to explore, a place to take a country walk or simply somewhere to picnic, every lake has something different beside its shore, and even when the scenery is less attractive than usual, the antics of people, water birds and animals are entertaining.

Something for everyone and every boat

Whether you have a sailing yacht, a tiny trailer boat, or a motor cruiser, you will find a waterway to suit your boat somewhere. Regardless of your interests; nature, history, gourmet eating, city life, there will be a place to satisfy your needs and those of your companions. Whether you are a lifelong cruiser or a boating beginner, there are waterways to suit your experience, from challenging passages along mighty rivers to tideless, sheltered waters which are perfect places to learn to sail.

Inland waterway cruising makes extended visits to nations' capitals affordable (imagine what it would cost to rent a cottage in a Paris suburb), and we've found that there is no better way of learning about the culture and customs of a country, and meeting its people, than by cruising its canals and rivers. Nothing could be further from the world of the average tourist, where chain hotel rooms in Saudi hardly differ from those in Swansea. On waterways you moor by cottages and fall into conversation (even if it is mainly in sign language) when the owner comes out to admire your boat, or tell you where to buy bread. You go to local markets and suss out the best places for bargains and – whether you are in Birmingham, Brussels or Bengtsfors – you can guarantee that you'll be able to sample unusual food and drink.

Getting started

In the first edition of *European Waterways*, we said that people who cruise inland waterways usually fall into one of two main categories: those on holiday;

and those who have sold house and home, bought the biggest, best equipped boat they could afford and gone off on a cruise without end. It was also mentioned that we had found a way of enjoying extensive inland cruising, without ripping up all our roots; by cruising to a new region, exploring it, then leaving the boat there for several months, until it was time to go off again. At that time, the book also highlighted that our 'no fixed abode' approach to keeping a boat inland had not been expensive, because each time we wanted to leave it we had been able to find a less than fashionable marina, or a small boatyard, to accommodate the vessel at very reasonable cost.

Today, we meet more and more people who are cruising in similar stages but, unfortunately, in several regions it is no longer quite as simple and inexpensive as it used to be. This is particularly true of southern France, close to the Mediterranean, where a combination of the increased popularity of inland cruising and sailing yacht owners seeking a winter home, has resulted in a shortage of berths. Last winter, we asked the owners of a Med bound yacht why they had chosen to moor during winter in Toulouse's marina, rather than at the warmer end of the Canal Entre-deux-Mers. 'Because friends told us they were fighting for berths over there,' was the reply. So, if you want to cruise in fits and starts, advance planning is now essential.

Even if you do decide on a permanent life afloat, you still don't need to sell up, or get hocked up, because a very ordinary boat can be made into a pleasant inland cruiser. In fact, spending a lot of money will not necessarily ensure that you acquire the perfect 'go anywhere' boat. During our wanderings, we have met people who bought boats at £40 000, £60 000 and even £100 000 plus, which were by no means ideal. On the other hand, we have cruised thousands of kilometres in a boat that was fifteen years old when we bought it, cost a fraction of those sums, and has been a superb sea and inland waterway boat.

That first cruise inland

We need to explode one of those, oft repeated, inland waterway myths – the one which advises newcomers to this sort of cruising to 'start off in small waterways, where there is little commercial traffic'!

As a general rule, small waterways have less space for passing and overtaking, more blind bends, shallower water, less well-maintained banks, more swing and lift bridges and fewer manned locks than their larger counter-parts. In other words, a far greater work load, which means far more stress. As to commercial traffic, we can positively assure you that travelling among barges is a whole lot easier than travelling among pleasure craft. Every bargee has passed a test; moreover, he is earning his living and cannot afford to have his vessel out of action, lose his licence, or risk his no claims bonus, because of a mishap involving another vessel. He will, therefore, be motoring in a competent and sensible manner. Conversely, the pleasure boat user will be in holiday mood and may be a hirer with no previous boating experience. Damaging his boat, or yours, would cause him some inconvenience, but it would not affect the way he earns his living.

Don't get into the tourist trap

We strongly recommend that if you want to visit an inland waterway that is described as 'one of Holland's, Wales', France's... most picturesque waterways', you avoid bank holidays and high season, when you can scarcely see scenery for superstructure.

Tourist brochures often give another clue to waterways that beginners should avoid in high season by marking hire boat bases. In France, which has a compulsory 'driving' test for resident boatowners, there are special arrangements for hirers in tourist regions. In Germany, non-residents may hire boats without

Some of Europe's most beautiful scenery is to be found around its inland waterways.

having a licence, but residents may not. Consequently, popular Dutch areas like Friesland and the Vecht attract a lot of unqualified German hirers. So, if there are a lot of hire bases, then in July and August many of the canal/river users may never have driven a boat before, and when you're approaching your first lock, the last thing you want for company is someone who knows even less than you do.

The Scandinavian canals are among the rare exceptions to the rule that beautiful 'for tourist use only' canals will be overcrowded in peak holiday periods and the Swedes say, 'If we find an island with another boat, we find another island.' We have cruised the Dalsland Canal in mid-August and, in over 250 kms cruising, never shared a lock with another cruiser.

Matching boat and waterway

We've met people who tried inland cruising once and said, 'Never again'. Some were put off by venturing onto an overcrowded waterway in peak holiday time, the rest had their first experience in a boat which was unsuitable for the waterway they decided to cruise. Even experienced sea-goers, when inland for the first time, should expect to find the workload higher than they've been used to, simply because so many things are different.

A modern, wide-bodied, flybridge cruiser, with its spacious accommodation, shallow draft and excellent viewing platform, might seem to be an ideal 'go anywhere' canal boat, especially as it can get you quickly over the sea to your chosen cruising ground. Certainly, there are few places that you couldn't take such a boat, but the inexperienced should avoid flat, windswept regions. Approaching Sloten in Friesland one day, we watched a German crew struggling to moor a hired flybridge cruiser in a crowded waterway. With that marvellous viewing platform acting as a sail, and little underwater hull to resist, no amount of bow thruster whine, multi-lingual curses and engine revving could get them near the quay – and, in trying, they bumped one boat and narrowly missed two more. In that particular tourist region the incident was merely embarrassing – even amusing to most onlookers – but in one of Holland's busy and equally windswept commercial canals, the consequences of such a lack of control could have been serious. If you own one of these boats, you would be wise to start your inland adventures in more sheltered UK rivers, then progress to French and Belgian canals, which are usually protected by wind-breaking trees, before venturing into exposed areas of Holland.

Friesland is criss-crossed by tiny canals, interspersed with fairly large meers, but the snag is that most of those meers are exceedingly shallow. Marked channels have been dredged across them, which most boats have to use, so things get very overcrowded. To get maximum enjoyment from a Friesland visit you need a shallow-draft boat which can explore the areas barred to most sea cruisers. The typical Broads cruiser (or similar river boat) would be very much at home there and equally suitable for many other quiet canal explorations.

How fit are you?

Another factor to consider is your physical fitness. Inland waterway cruising is not usually arduous (we've met several 80 year olds happily cruising the Continent) but, if you are not very fit, tackling a flight of eleven hand-operated locks in a morning, or dragging a 70-foot (21 metre) narrow boat round several tight bends, could be a bit exhausting. Keeping to bigger and better maintained waterways will make manoeuvring easier and will add to the odds that locks will either be manned or electronically controlled, or that you can share hand work with the crew of another boat.

Sailing inland

Some people might find it hard to believe that there are canals where tall masted, deep keel sailing boats are completely at home, but its true. Between 1803 and 1822, Thomas Telford turned the Great Glen and its lochs Lochy, Oich and Ness into the majestic Caledonian Canal of today; a 96.6km (60 miles) waterway linking Inverness to Fort William. It offers spectacular scenery, abundant wildlife and can accommodate craft with a draught of 4.11m (13ft 6in) and a mast height of 35m (115ft); 27.4m (89ft 9in) if you exit at Inverness.

Sweden's Lake Vanern, with its 22 000 islands and islets, is a perfect sailing ground in its own right and the entrance to four canals of a similar type to the Caledonian; the Trolhatte, Gota, Saffle and our personal favourite, the 250 kms long Dalsland. This canal was opened in 1868, so that logs could be more easily brought down to iron works and paper mills. Water depth in the locks is 1.8 metres and, in between the short canalised sections, there are vast, idyllic lakes to sail and an endless variety of moorings; from small pleasure harbours in quaint towns to remote places where you may encounter all manner of wildlife, from beavers to bears. Only overhead power cables limit mast heights to between 12 and 20 metres, depending on the section you are cruising. Norway's similar 'log driving' canal, the Telemark, is another favourite of ours that winds its way deep into the mountains, through truly spectacular countryside.

Holland's Zeeland, and the meers and rivers that lead inland, are near ideal motor cruising or sailing regions if you avoid holiday periods, when pontoons can get stacked ten alongside and four abreast! Apart from the West Schelde (which can largely be avoided by taking the Walcheren Canal, from Flushing to Veere), navigating the estuary areas is not demanding and several of the meers are protected by tree-lined banks. This means that you can often find a safe sailing area, even in rougher weather. If the wind does become too strong and you have to dash for shelter, it will almost certainly be in an ancient former fishing port. These historic small towns always justify more than a brief exploration.

The majority of bridges in Zeeland are well over any normal mast height and the meers lead into vast rivers where you can still sail. From there, you can continue inland, though it would be wiser to motor in the much-frequented main canals. Further afield, you'll find that many Dutch canals can be used by sailing vessels, with the mast in position. If you do discover that you need to get it down before you can proceed along your chosen route, that is unlikely to be a problem: almost every Dutch canal or riverside town has a Crane Street (the street leading to a crane where you can get your mast taken down).

Trailer boats

Even a tiny trailer boat could be a very good choice for a first inland cruising boat, if you are able to take your holidays in spring or autumn, because it enables you to explore far and wide from day one.

Clearly, very small boats are not recommended for venturing onto the Continent's main commercial waterways, but popular places in the sun can be a joy to cruise off season. France's Canal du Midi is quiet in early spring, and even when the snow is still capping the distant Pyrénées, you may find all you need wear is a swimsuit. Even in late September, excellent weather can often be experienced on the Sarthe, Mayenne and other canals of the Loire region and your trailer boat will take you to places other cruisers cannot reach. Even if your boat does not have any accommodation, you can still enjoy a holiday in this part of France, where camp sites to pitch your tent can be found by the canal and river banks.

Avoid the rush hours

Of course, although we have said that newcomers will be more comfortable in larger canals, we are not suggesting that you should start your inland waterway cruising with a voyage up the Waal, or an exploration of one of Europe's three busiest river exit ports (Rotterdam, Ghent and Antwerpen). Like any 'road' system, the commercial continental inland waterway system has its speed limits, its busy and quiet stretches, even its traffic hold ups and rush hours. The IJ, near Amsterdam station, is a good example. In a one kilometre stretch, several ferries ply continuously across, whilst water taxis take fares up and down river. Add to that river boats taking tourists to see the sights, plus barges using this as a through route, and you'll realise it's no place for a beginner to be at times when many people are using the river as a route to and from work! A visit to the reference library to examine some town plan maps will help you plan a route to avoid such places. If the river/canal running through a town has a mass of basins or loops going off it, it is a place to avoid until you've got some inland waterway experience.

Tourist information

To help you appraise the myriad cruising ground options, and choose one that will suit both you and your boat, you will need general waterway maps as well as local tourist brochures. Most countries have a Tourist Information Office, which will send brochures, and sources of maps are given in Appendix B. At this stage, you don't need anything detailed – just the sort of map that gives waterway sizes and depths, such as *European Inland Waterways* published in 1994 by the Economic Commission for Europe (ISBN 92-1-016-299-4), for the Continent, and for the UK, general maps indicating broad and narrow waterways which you can obtain from British Waterways and other UK authorities.

Many charming Dutch towns provide free moorings for pleasure craft passing through.

A good starting point

The canals of Flanders, the area behind the French and Belgian Channel ports, are a natural place to start continental explorations and a good place to learn inland waterway techniques, because the majority are quite large and the smaller ones are not heavily frequented by barges or pleasure craft. (A census in July 1993 recorded just 300 vessels on the 680 kilometres of waterways in the Nord Pas-de-Calais.)

Voies Navigables de France (see Appendix B for address) will send you an excellent Northern France/Belgium canal map (enclose an International Reply Coupon), and studying it at the planning stage will enable even those with a deeper-draft vessel, such as a sailing yacht, to select a route where excess draft is not a great embarrassment. However, after a prolonged dry spell it would be prudent to take local advice before venturing into some of the more rural rivers. Paradoxically, a prolonged wet spell can also cause problems, since silt (and other debris) can sweep down from upstream areas to reduce water depth.

Masts can be lowered at Channel ports, at reasonable cost, before setting off to explore this 'nearest to home' part of the Continent. On waterways like the Canal de Calais and l'Aa from Gravelines, those with deeper-draft vessels will need to keep a sharp lookout for obstructions if they have to go to the side. On larger canals, like the Dunkerque–Escaut waterway, there will be no worries about water depth, so, apart from tripping over the mast, when you suddenly discover that you need to moor on the 'other' side of the lock, canal cruising will have become relaxing. You can also solve that problem by exiting at the port you entered and having the mast stored there whilst you go inland.

Hire before you buy

If you are thinking of buying a boat for inland cruising and are undecided about whether you want to have a narrow boat, a river boat or a 'go anywhere' cruiser, a few holidays afloat could be the answer. Many hire firms offer weekend rates and some even do day hire so, without spending a fortune, you could try various types of cruising. In any case, it's better to spend a few hundred pounds on boat hire, and then decide it isn't for you, than to spend a few thousand on a boat and come to the same conclusion!

When choosing a hire company, look for evidence that the boats are well maintained – you don't want your holiday spoiled by breakdowns. If you are a beginner, ask a lot of questions about what pre-cruise tuition is offered – if you suspect it might be inadequate go elsewhere. Finally, study the hire contract carefully to check exactly what you are paying for. Some companies' rates are for virtually everything you need, right down to maps and guides, others have a basic price plus extras. It's something to watch out for.

UK canals

The commercial UK canal system, which was developed mainly in the late eighteenth and early nineteenth centuries, has always been a predominantly 'narrow gauge' network. Many of the locks, bridges and aqueducts were constructed to accept narrow boats, mainly up to 70 feet (21 metres) long and 7 feet (2 metres) wide, but some canals were larger and had locks that would take two narrow boats, strapped side by side. Again, we would recommend that any newcomer to narrow boating should start off in the bigger canals. Entering your very first lock with feet to spare is a lot easier than coming in with inches to spare. Having more room will also make it easier to learn the art of getting a long thin boat round a tight corner! Of course, owners of conventional cruisers (apart from some very small ones) can only use the larger sections of the UK network.

Classification of UK canals

Original canal profiles vary, so British Waterways have not been able to standardise in their maintenance and upgrading programme. However, their target has been a minimum depth of 3 feet (0.9 metres) on cruising waterways, with dredging carried out to 4H feet (1.35 metres) where possible. Waterways have been classified as being to Navigation Standards 1, 2 and 3 and Environs Standards A, B and C. In setting the standards, safety of the public, users and canal staff has been a prime consideration – after that, market forces take over. The Environs Standards relate to quality of surroundings, customer service, user facilities etc and refer to specific sites or stretches of waterway. Leaving aside things like the frequency of effluent disposal points, some of the important differences between these standards worked out for waterways are the cruising times between marinas, popular moorings, major attractions and turning areas. The Navigation Standards usually apply to a complete waterway or ring:

Navigation Standard 1 Very busy waterways with, on average, over 10 000 boat passages per year. Cruising time: approximately 1 hour.

Navigation Standard 2 Waterways with, on average, between 1000 and 10 000 boat passages per year. About 90 per cent of British Waterways-controlled waterways come into this category. Cruising time: approximately 2 hours.

Navigation Standard 3 Little-used waterways with, on average, less than 1000 boat passages per year. Cruising time: approximately 4 hours.

Standard 1 and Standard 2 waterways have clearly identifiable level areas, with hard edges and mooring bollards (for landing crew at lock/bridge approaches etc), with sufficient water depth to allow typical canal boats to moor tight to the edge. These moorings have room for three boats on Standard 1 waterways and at least one (minimum mooring length 80 feet (24 metres)) on Standard 2. Standard 3 waterways have level areas for landing crew at lock/bridge approaches etc, with room for one boat of the type that uses the waterway. There is sufficient water depth to allow typical canal boats to moor within 2 feet (0.6) metres of the edge.

Except in river navigations at times of flood/drought, there should be sufficient water supply to limit closures to 1 in 20 years on Standard 1 waterways; 1 in 10 years on Standard 2 waterways; 1 in 5 years on Standard 3 waterways. Following a report, serious navigational obstructions should be removed within 24 hours on Standard 1 waterways; 48 hours on Standard 2 waterways; and 7 days on Standard 3 waterways.

On Standard 1 and Standard 2 waterways, routine stoppages at any one point should be restricted to periods between November and mid-March, (excluding Christmas/New Year) and should not exceed 3 weeks (Standard 1), 6 weeks (Standard 2), or 12 weeks (Standard 3). On Standard 2 and Standard 3 waterways, there may be stoppages possible throughout the year if readily available alternative routes exist. In all cases, there may be exceptions on rivers to allow work to be carried out in low flows. Except for unforeseen events, major work stoppages on Standard 1 waterways are confined to the November to mid-March period and kept to the minimum achievable by reasonable use of resources, but stoppages and timings on Standard 3 waterways are arranged to achieve minimum cost solution.

Major lock flights and key locks are manned at all peak times, by trained staff, on Standard 1 waterways. Staff may be available, during the normal working day, on Standard 2 waterways. On Standard 3 waterways, when lock flights are manned it is primarily for water control purposes rather than to assist boaters.

Obviously, the chances of problems, such as running aground or having your holiday ruined because the canal has been closed, are greater on Standard 3 waterways. On the other hand, Standard 1 waterways are likely to be very crowded during peak holiday periods.

Standard 1 waterways are dredged to original canal depth less 4 in (10 cm), or more than 1.3 times the draft of a standard vessel (whichever is least). The width of the navigable channel (level with the bottom of a standard hull) is more than 3.5 times the width of that hull.

Standard 2 waterways are dredged to original canal depth less 12 in (30 cm), or more than 1.2 times the draft of a standard vessel (whichever is least). The width of the navigable channel (level with the bottom of a standard hull) is more than 3 times the width of the hull.

Standard 3 waterways are dredged to more than the draft of a standard vessel. The width of the navigable channel (level with the bottom of a standard hull) is generally more than twice the width of that hull but, in some places, passing points may be needed.

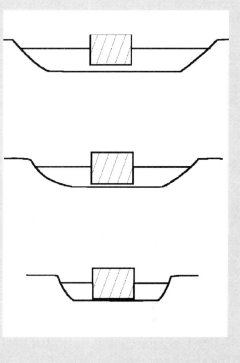

Fig 1.1 UK classification of waterways.

2

Buying an inland waterway boat

Although there is a waterway somewhere to suit just about any sort of boat, if you want to have the freedom to roam throughout the continent's vast network, you need to consider choosing the right boat for the purpose. In the past, there's been an 'any old boat will do' and 'what do we need qualifications for' attitude to inland waterway cruising. A few decades ago, when some barges were still horse drawn and a 1300 ton vessel was gargantuan, that may have been OK. Today, on Europe's busy waterway thoroughfares, 1300 tonners are commonplace and vessels 175 metres long, thundering along at almost 20 kph, are not uncommon, so a 'gung-ho' approach is no longer acceptable. There will always be someone who'll tell you – quite proudly – that they've been everywhere, in their entirely unsuitable boat, without having a clue about any rules and regulations; but that's about as sensible as boasting that they drove a moped up the M1 without a driving licence!

Permanent protection, like this rope fender, brings peace of mind.

Design and construction are paramount

The fundamental criteria to bear in mind when you are considering buying any boat, is that design and construction are of paramount importance. A well designed, correctly engineered older boat, which handles well, will function far better than an ill designed newer one, which is less well constructed and not so responsive.

We would even go a stage further and say that you should not say 'no' to a boat because it has not been well cared for, as a correctly engineered vessel can tolerate a lot of neglect before it deteriorates. When we first saw the *vlet*, which has taken us along thousands of trouble-free kilometres, it looked decidedly tatty, with faded paint, peeling varnish and some bent stanchions. However, it had been designed and built by one of Holland's prestigious yards (CC Bruys of Bergen-op-Zoom) using only top-quality materials and components; and when we looked beyond the general air of neglect, we discovered that the things that matter were still in excellent condition. Castrol analysed the oil and found nothing to suggest wear in the Daf engine and a sonic test revealed that the zinc-coated steel hull plates were as thick as the day the boat was launched.

Size

Most people go for the biggest boat they can afford, but there is a downside to this. For example, you can't turn the longer narrow boats in narrow UK canals, so if your mooring is four hours' cruising from the nearest turning point, you can never have a short cruise on a long boat. In certain parts of the UK the canals are narrow, so you should ensure that the boat you want to buy will not restrict your cruising by being too wide.

Our 10 metre *vlet* was a little bit small for two couples, from the point of view of moving about inside. Nevertheless, we have thoroughly enjoyed our cruising and, for one couple, it would have been near perfect.

The UK system dictates your choice

Between 1906 and 1909, a Royal Commission studied both British and overseas waterway systems, with a view to deciding how the British system could be changed to provide facilities to transport larger cargos over greater distances. Their multi-volume report included a paragraph that pointed out that, Britain apart, the entire civilised world was developing integrated road, rail and water-way systems, in public ownership. They therefore recommended that Britain should adopt the same well-proven policy and enlarge the major waterway trunk routes.

Had the Royal Commission had its way, owners of conventional cruisers would now be able to cruise the length and breadth of Britain, for the initial stage of their plan was the upgrading of trunk waterways between the Rivers Severn, Thames, Mersey and Humber to a minimum of 100 ton barge dimensions. Alas, these changes, which would have greatly reduced costs to British industry, were never implemented; so if you want to explore the entire UK canal network, you must have a narrow boat which British Waterways bylaws defines as 'a vessel having a beam of less than 7 ft 6 ins (2.3 metres)'.

Engines

Torque is all important

The one thing that any good canal boat needs, whether it is to cruise tiny UK canals or mighty international rivers, is a marine engine with plenty of low-down torque. On engine specification sheets, you will usually find that figures of maximum power and maximum torque are given. Data sheets for older engines usually express power as 'brake horse power' and torque in 'pounds feet'. More modern engine outputs are usually expressed in kilowatts of power and Newton metres or kilogram metres of torque.

In advertisements, engine outputs are nearly always quoted as power outputs, but in truth power is almost irrelevant on an inland waterway boat. It is the torque – the ability to twist your propeller – which is all important. This, above all else, will decide whether your narrow boat can stop before it hits that bridge, whether it can smoothly pull away from a pub-side quay, whether your cruiser can quickly get out of the way when double locks disgorge several hundred thousand tons of shipping beside you, and whether it can easily go up the Rhone.

One often repeated, but nevertheless misleading, statement is 'you need a 10 knot boat to go up the Rhine'. In fact, our *vlet* is absolutely flat out at 8.5 knots, with the engine turning over at 2200 revs, but we have never had a problem going up the Rhine without exceeding the 1800 revs that we prefer not to use as a maximum. That is because the Daf engine develops almost 200 lbs/ft torque at only 1000 revs, peaking at 228 lbs/ft at 1700 rpm, and the boat has a 2:1 reduction gearbox which, except for some transmission losses, doubles the available torque at the propeller.

If you are not mechanically minded, and therefore a bit confused about this matter of power and torque, think about a car. A 600 hp Formula 1 car can do over 200 mph, but it would not pull a 2 ton trailer up a hill. An 80 hp diesel van might be flat out at 80 mph, but it would easily cope with hauling the trailer.

Long-stroke engines

Don't let anyone convince you that because your boat has an old engine, it will either be unsuitable or unreliable. Older engines (or engines based on older designs) are often more suitable for inland waterway cruising than modern ones.

Most marine engines are based on car or commercial vehicle engines, and in the days when there were fewer high speed roads, engines were designed to be efficient at the low engine revolutions needed on twisty roads. That meant they had a lot of torque at low revolutions, something that to a considerable extent was achieved by having a long stroke and a heavy flywheel. The advent of a fast road network meant that priorities changed and produced a need for engines capable of propelling a vehicle at sustained high speeds, which required a lot of power at higher revolutions. This resulted in engines with short strokes and light flywheels, therefore not much low-down torque. So, most modern marine units are best suited to propelling a cruiser at higher speeds than those used on inland waterways. You'll see what we mean, if you compare the published torque figures for the 2178 ccs BMC Commander, designed around 60 years ago, and a comparably sized modern unit (see Fig 2.1).

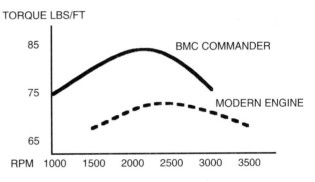

There is another benefit to having an older-design, long-stroke engine. A long-stroke eng ine can have a longer piston and longer pistons can have more piston rings, including two sets of oil control rings. For a number of reasons, this configuration is better for an engine that is

Fig 2.1 Published figures for the 2178 cc BMC Commander and a comparable modern engine.

going to spend much of its life at near tickover speeds.

If you are unhappy about any boat's handling, pulling away and stopping characteristics, the first thing you should examine is its engine torque. If that is the problem, there are a number of ways you may be able to improve things without fitting a new engine. It might be possible to 'back the torque curve' by modifying the characteristics of the fuel injection pump or you might be able to have a reduction gear fitted to the gearbox, which will enable your engine to turn a much larger propeller more effectively.

Reliability

Diesel engines are incredibly long lived. If you give them uncontaminated fuel, the right amount of oil in the sump, and don't over-rev or overheat them, then – even with worn injectors, or valves that could do with a regrind – they will usu- ally run and keep on running. When we were considering buying our *vlet*, we knew it was already 15 years old, so we phoned Daf to ask about the life expectancy of the engine. 'Indefinite,' they said. 'Indefinite?' we queried. 'What does that mean?' The answer was, 'There is no reason why it should not go on working forever.'

Most boat engines run at much lower revolutions than their road going equivalents, so are under stressed. The more stressed car and lorry versions do thousands of miles, year after year, so there really is no reason why the life of their underused and under stressed marine counterparts should not be 'indefinite'. Nevertheless, when buying a boat or an engine, longevity should be considered. Some older engines, for example, have six lives (four rebores and two relines) but many more modern units do not.

One engine or two?

There seems to be a belt and braces attitude among many pleasure boat owners that two engines are better than one, but because of the basic reliability of diesel engines, breakdowns are rare. If your installation has been so badly maintained that one engine stops running, what is there to say that its partner won't follow suit? In a way a twin installation could be regarded as a drawback because maintenance is more expensive – not because of the engines, but because of everything that goes with them: starter motors, stern gear, cooling systems etc. Also, a second engine takes up room and, on an extended canal cruise, you never seem to have enough room for everything you want to take with you. Another snag, where beginners are concerned, is that two sets of controls means more to think about. If you are still unconvinced about one engine being as good an option as two, ask yourself how many fishing boats and barges you've seen with twin engines? If the people who earn their living with their boats rarely fit two engines, it's a good indication that one is the best option!

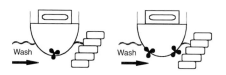

Fig 2.2 With a twin-engined installation, you must take extra care near banks.

In some circumstances, twin engines can make manoeuvring easier, but to get the best out of a 'one in reverse, one forward' technique, you need experience. In any case, that technique is only really effective when the propellers are widely spaced, and having the props wide apart can introduce another snag when you are motoring (or about to moor) near a sloping canal bank (see Fig 2.2).

One of the big attractions of canal cruising is stopping where and when you want to, perhaps calling at a riverside pub, mooring for lunch in attractive countryside, or stopping to explore a quaint old river port. This means that anything that makes you think 'Can I moor here without risking damage?' is a major drawback, so given the choice of single- or twin-engined boats, with the same torque to weight ratio, we would opt for the single-engined version.

Wing engines

Another engine option is the wing and main combination, which we have used for many years. We use our main 120 hp Daf for manoeuvring, lock work and punching against strong flows or tides, and our Sabb (yes it is Sabb, not Saab) 18 hp wing engine for much of our cruising. The 1100 cc Sabb produces an incredible 83 ft/lbs of propeller torque at only 1550 revs and, providing you choose an equally 'torquey' wing engine, you will have that belt and braces security – which is certainly reassuring at sea – without some of the twin-engined drawbacks. A small wing engine doesn't take up as much room as a second main engine and, provided you can moor with the non-engined side next to the bank, you are unlikely to damage a propeller on a sloping canal side.

The drawback is that your boat will have a lopsided turning ability when you are using the wing engine alone. On our first journey down the sleepy Canal de Furnes, we were lazily enjoying sunshine and scenery when we discovered that the gentle bend we had started to negotiate was tightening up and the boat had no intention of following it round. We were only saved from a minor encounter with a stone wall by the fact that the main Daf started instantly and the boat reversed quickly.

In spite of that we are still fans of main/wing engines, if only because of the low fuel bills we have when using the Sabb. However, since that episode we now start the Daf and leave it ticking over if we suspect that an unseen hazard may lie ahead! If you do go for this combination, choose your wing engine carefully. Again, high torque is the main consideration, but there are other factors to consider. Some small engines, like our Norwegian-made Sabb (which is very popular with coastal fishermen all over Europe), have a hand start capability. This is very useful because, provided the engine is fitted with a 12 or 24 volt alternator, it can be used to charge flat batteries and thus start the main engine.

Diesel versus petrol

By now, you will have noted that every engine we have mentioned has been a diesel engine. That is no accident; we simply do not like the idea of having an inboard petrol engine in a boat. With diesel, a dripping fuel union or a broken delivery pipe would be unlikely to cause anything worse than a messy bilge and a nasty smell, but in the case of petrol the same problems could lead to an inferno.

Gearboxes and controls

In the case of gearboxes and controls, the single-lever type of control is simplest to operate. One lever performs the twin functions of putting the boat into gear, and opening the engine throttle. The less experienced you are, then the less things you have to fumble around with the better – so this system is a plus. The most suitable gearbox is a hydraulic unit (similar to many car automatic transmissions) because, with a correctly adjusted engine tickover speed, when the gear is engaged the boat (or car) does not move forward until the throttle is opened further. If you have to put up with separate controls for the gearbox and throttle, you may be able to make life easier by repositioning them closer together.

Hull strength and shape

Materials

After the power train, the next most important factor for that ideal canal boat is the hull type and material. Aluminium is probably the least suitable hull material as it tends to split under impact, and repairs require specialised welding equipment not often found in the average canalside boatyard. Steel has to be the favourite material, because it

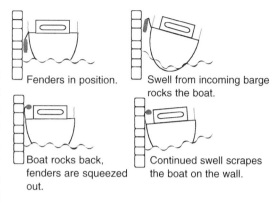

Fenders in position.

Swell from incoming barge rocks the boat.

Boat rocks back, fenders are squeezed out.

Continued swell scrapes the boat on the wall.

Fig 2.3 Damage is possible in a lock even when a boat is fendered.

can best withstand the bumps and scrapes that – however experienced you are – are bound to occur from time to time. Choosing between GRP and wood is more difficult. The GRP boat is likely to be completely watertight, except perhaps for a stern gland drip, but the gel coat would be easily damaged by scraping on concrete lock sides, allowing water to penetrate into the structure. Fig 2.3 shows how even a well-fendered boat can get scraped in locks.

A solidly built new, or newish, wooden boat would be a close second to steel, as it would stand a fair amount of knocking about. However, most wooden boats date back to the 1960s, or earlier, and a hull that seemed sound

A steel hull, sloping bow and powerful engine make the Dutch vlet *an excellent 'go anywhere' inland cruising boat.*

enough in gentle use may not take kindly to the jolts and bumps that are an inevitable part of weeks of continual lock dockings. Another snag is that wood's tendency to rot is greater in fresh water than in salt. One yacht broker in Holland told us that most of the Dutch, who are the greatest inland waterway enthusiasts in the world, have a positive horror of wooden boats. Certainly, sailing yachts apart, anything other than steel boats is an uncommon sight in Holland's canals and rivers.

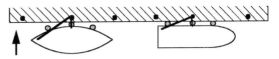

A round boat and a flat-sided boat are secured in a lock, using stern and centre lines, attached to the same bollard. This is a deep lock standard technique which will be described in a later chapter.

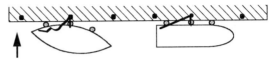

The wash of an incoming barge (in direction of arrow) will tend to push the stern of the rounded vessel into the wall. When the wash reaches the flat-sided vessel, it will not be affected.

Fig 2.4 Comparison of hull shapes.

Another advantage of a wellconstructed steel boat, or a massively built wooden one, is its weight (our 10 metre *vlet* weighs 10 tons). Heavy boats are less easily rocked about, provided that most of that weight is low down, so nights spent lying against the bank tend to be more comfortable, because the wash of passing boats doesn't disturb you as much. For the same reason, a reasonable draft (at least 1 metre) is desirable, unless you mainly want to explore very shallow waters. Boats with little draft are more easily rocked and more easily pushed sideways by wind and passing vessels.

Profiles

Some hull plans and profiles are more suitable than others. A boat with rounded sides is harder to keep positioned in locks and more difficult to fender. The ideal boat for handling in locks would have slab sides, like a barge, but a cruiser of that shape wouldn't look very nice, so you need to compromise.

Medieval river boats, similar to the *bacoves* of France's Audormarois, have always had bows that are decidedly sloping. The original 'design' came about

Vessel with upright bow is about to contact the bank, before it is near enough for someone to step off.

Vessel with curved bow can get near enough for someone to step off.

Fig 2.5 Bow shapes.

because, in those early times, planks could most easily be formed to that shape. However, it proved to be the ideal bow for nosing into banks and stepping off at the front – so ideal that even today visitors to the Audormarois can see near-identical vessels being used to tend 'island' market gardens, surrounded by tiny canals. There are many occasions when you will want to nose into a bank and step off, and a sloping bow shape will make this much easier (Fig 2.5).

On deck

Some boats have wider sidedecks than others, and some have no sidedecks at all. A narrow sidedeck, or none at all, increases the space with standing headroom, but the drawback can be difficulty in quickly moving from one end of the boat to the other (eg in a narrow boat with cluttered interior). If there are just two of you, locking and docking manoeuvres will be more difficult on a vessel that does not have wide sidedecks.

Keel cooling

Our last main recommend-ation about basic hull design is to go for keel cooling if you have a choice. Keel cooling is a cooling system whereby water is not drawn in from the outside and it is worthwhile because most canals are full of plastic bags, leaves and other floating debris waiting to block a water intake. The only drawback to keel cooling is

| Boat is moored. | Passing barge creates wash. | Fender jumps out, keel hits cill as boat rocks back. |

Fig 2.6 Keel cooling.

the possibility of damaging the keel on canal sides, or the cills of some commercial moorings. So it's worth the extra care needed to avoid situations such as that shown in Fig 2.6.

Handling

Narrow boats

We've regularly heard narrow boat users say 'I can't do anything with it at low speed'. Given that narrow boats never go very fast, and that manoeuvres like locking, turning and tunnelling require even slower speeds, this problem needs addressing. One of the best ways to do this is to study continental barges, which are similar in shape and proportions to narrow boats (a 300 ton barge has a length/beam ratio of 7.6:1, a 3000 ton convoy 12.5:1). Every day regardless of wind, tide, current, or other impediment, barge crews of man and wife squeeze these boats into locks, moor them in gaps barely longer than the vessel, and they do it entirely without fuss.

If you watch barges manoeuvring in confined spaces, the first thing you'll notice is that everything is done very, very slowly and engines are turning very, very slowly. This confirms our earlier comments that an abundance of low-down torque transmitted by a suitable gearbox and propeller is the first essential. Studying the rear of a barge also gives other clues about factors which improve controllability.

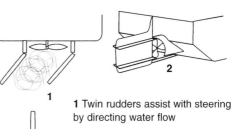

1 Twin rudders assist with steering by directing water flow

2 and **3** Foils on the rudder and a cowl over the propeller also help to direct water flow. The cowl can also reduce cavitation noise.

Fig 2.7 Features which could improve steering

Several narrow boat drivers have told us that they have found it easier to control a boat with an outboard engine than one with an inboard engine. The reason is that a swivelling outboard allows the propeller to push away the water in the right direction, thus acting rather like a thruster. The snag is that few outboard engines have much low-down torque, so fitting one means trading a benefit for a drawback.

However, twin rudders (a feature on some barges) direct the water flow in a similar way to an outboard, and if you are having a narrow boat built, this is an option to discuss with the builder. It may also be possible to improve the handling of your existing narrow boat by adding one, or both, of these barge features. Both the propeller cowl and the rudder hydrofoils help to ensure that the motive force from the propeller (ie water flow) is not dissipated. The cowl also helps to reduce cavitation noise.

Bow thrusters

A good bow thruster makes manoeuvring easier in any boat, though bow thrusters are a palliative with regard to handling problems, rather than a cure. They are not cheap, and one snag in fitting a thruster to an inland waterway boat is the possibility of weed entering its tunnel. Another drawback is that heavy boats need powerful thrusters, and powerful thrusters consume more watts. Frequent use of an electric bow thruster, eg in a heavily locked section, could potentially flatten your batteries.

Layout considerations

Your final choice of vessel will, to a large extent, depend on your personal views about the way a boat looks and the accommodation you want, but various features have pros and cons.

Wheelhouse versus open cockpit

Wheelhouses give better bad weather comfort and make good dining rooms. The disadvantages are that the helmsman can't sunbathe whilst going along (though sometimes that is an advantage) and is a bit cut off from those on deck; and in locks it is less easy for the helmsman to give a hand with lines. On balance, the wheelhouse must be the best option, because it makes the boat more secure.

Flybridge

Excessive windage has already been mentioned as a flybridge cruiser snag. Another drawback is that, when steering from the flybridge, it is almost impossible to lend a hand in locks and whilst mooring. The obvious advantage is better viewing and a spacious alfresco dining area.

Aft cabin versus rear cockpit

Having used an aft cabin boat for so long, we'd definitely go for that layout. With two couples on board, both have privacy. If there is just one couple, they live in the saloon and use the aft cabin as a bedroom. A couple with children can put them to bed aft, and then go on chatting to some of those passing acquaintances one meets on the canals. Another disadvantage of the rear cockpit is that you

Other features to consider

Dining/leisure area Ideally, this should be to one side of the saloon rather than in the middle (unless you have a big boat), so that those who don't want to join in can still move about.

Loo/shower If possible this should be in a communal area, rather than in someone's cabin.

Opening windscreens and good saloon ventilation (you'll appreciate a draft in hot weather).

Large bitts (vertical deck fittings for attaching mooring lines) – much easier to use in locks.

Good storage space – for all that wine you'll want to buy in France.

Large water tanks – in parts of Holland, for example, you have to pay for water.

Rope fender, or rubber strake – for obvious reasons.

Some form of guard rail and lots of handholds are absolutely essential for safety, especially in locks.

Another point to consider when you are thinking of buying a boat is, 'How easy will it be to make modifications, or add equipment, at a later date?' (Read Chapter 3 on preparing the boat, and then check such things as: space for additional batteries, and underdeck access for securely attaching things like davits, extra bitts, stanchions etc.)

have a lot to peer round when entering locks, and it isn't so easy to handle the ropes with this layout.

Try before you buy

We once met an unhappy UK couple cruising in Holland who had purchased a boat from photographs and the specification sheet. It was a lovely vessel – spacious, well laid out, and in superb condition. Unfortunately, it also had a high-revving engine, was slow to respond to the helm, and nigh impossible to reverse in a straight line. In other words, a nightmare to manoeuvre in inland waterways.

The moral is that, whatever boat you are buying, you should insist on the opportunity to thoroughly test its handling. Good handling stems primarily from the right hull/engine configuration, so that is more important than anything else. You can add equipment, refit an interior etc, as and when you can afford it, but you can't do much to change a basically ill-designed hull. And if the engine isn't right, you are unlikely to be able to change it without major expense.

Dutch brokers

If you are looking for a cruiser and can't find the right boat at the right price in the UK, don't opt for second best until you have been to Holland. A visit need not be expensive (look for Kamer, Zimmer or Bed & Breakfast), and there is virtually no language barrier. We would be surprised if you met a yacht broker who did not speak English and, because there are huge numbers of boats to choose from, prices are competitive. Never accept that the asking price is the actual selling price.

You don't really need to contact Dutch brokers in advance because, wherever you go, there are almost certain to be several in a 30 kilometre radius, but, if you want to get lists in advance, the Dutch Maritime Federation (HISWA) (see Appendix B) will supply a list of member brokers. However, the best bargain may be the one that the broker didn't bother to tell you about, because it looks a bit downmarket. The Dutch, especially in north Holland, have very high standards about cosmetic finish, so boats with grubby paintwork and faded varnish can often be bought at bargain prices. And if you want to cruise continental waterways, buying in Holland has an added advantage – you don't have to cross the sea to get there!

Boat Safety Scheme

Finally, all boats using British inland waterways need to have a British Boat Safety Certificate before they can obtain a licence to use the waterways. Get a copy of the requirements from the waterway authorities listed in Appendix B before purchasing a boat which does not have a certificate.

Getting the boat ready

I don't know anyone who made their first long sea passage without fitting extra equipment, but I know several who have gone on their first inland waterway cruise without adding to their cruising inventory. Perhaps this is because, in the past, books have tended to imply that all you need on the canals are extra-long warps and some old tyres for fenders.

In fact, we don't use especially long ropes (even in 20 metre+ locks) and tyres are now banned almost everywhere. This is because they get ripped off in locks, sink, and then jam the mechanism, which delays commercial traffic. You may have heard people say 'Oh, don't bother about the ban on tyres, no-one pulls you up for having them.' That is usually true, but what these people don't realise is that, if you do lose one – and boats are often filmed in locks – the authorities will not hesitate to present you with a bill for sending divers down. This would tend to spoil a holiday, so raiding the local Kwikfit dump should not form part of your pre-cruise preparations!

To make space for stores, clothes etc, items that should be regarded as 'essential equipment' for a coastal cruise are often left behind on the grounds that 'We won't need that on canals'. In fact, sooner or later, you probably will! For example, snubbers (springy items – often rubber – put on mooring lines to prevent them snatching), are often forgotten yet there are many places where it might be hard to sleep without them. Examples are the Albert Canal, where 3000 ton barges thunder past at 15 kph+, Holland's Zwarte Water, where rushing up and down in speed boats is a regular evening pastime, and on the Norfolk Broads when inconsiderate hirers won't slow down. As you stow something, make a list of where it is; this will avoid having to turn out several lockers when you suddenly need mooring spikes, baked beans or anything else!

Essential equipment

Don't be put off inland waterway cruising because you can't afford to fit the expensive gadgets that the advertising hype says you simply *must* fit. Pressurised water systems, flow meters, inverters etc are nice to have, but they are not essential. In a way, the longer your cruise, the less you need such things, because after the first month your attitude to life will have changed. Everything will have slowed down, so it won't matter that you have to hand pump water rather than switching on an electric pump. Even the fact that the batteries are flat won't be a catastrophe. You'll just do some more exploring, whilst the local garage charges them.

The following are items which are essential for safe and comfortable cruising:

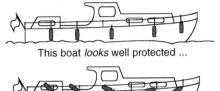

This boat *looks* well protected ...

Fenders

Locks are the biggest worry for beginners, and often hilarious for those spectators listening to the cries of 'We're going to hit' and 'Get another fender on', accompanied

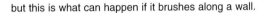

but this is what can happen if it brushes along a wall.

Fig 3.1 Fenders.

by frantic scurryings. A good fender system will do much to eliminate tensions. A big fat rope, or strake, plus plastic fenders, are best.

You sometimes come across antique locks restored and maintained to pristine condition, but spotless lock walls are not the norm. Most are rough, slimy and, in industrial areas, covered with pollutants, so shiny new fenders do not stay that way. We reserve a few clean ones for yacht club mooring, and use disreputable

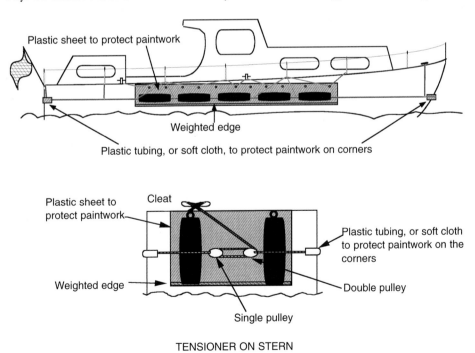

TENSIONER ON STERN

Fig 3.2 Permanent fendering for sides and stern.

examples whilst *en route*. When fitting out on a budget, ten scuffed and grubby secondhand fenders are a better buy than two new ones. Five fenders per side will protect most boats, but if you brush along a wall they can ride up, so permanent or semi-permanent protection is better (see Fig 3.1 and Fig 3.2).

Ladder

This is essential for getting up to some high quays, eg on the cheaper side of Bassin Ouest at Calais, you may not be adjacent to a quay ladder. It can also double as extra fender protection if you don't have a semi-permanent system. Hanging it over central fenders will help keep them in place, but it will tend to sway to and fro. You can minimise this by threading a rope through, but protect your boat's corners with a plastic tube or soft cloth.

Boarding plank

You will need this for getting ashore at sloping canal sides. With suitable holes drilled, it can also double as the fender protection plank (have the anti-slip strips inward) on the opposite side from the ladder (Fig 3.3).

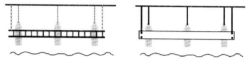

Ladder and boarding plank can also double as additional protection.

Fig 3.3 Boarding planks.

Boathooks

Keep two handy in locks, for use when you've got it wrong! They should be of a type which will float if dropped overboard and the hooks must not be made of steel or any other material which could cause sparks if, for example, you got too close to a fuel barge. One should be extra long or telescopic, and fitted with the type of end which can be used with your mooring loop (below). To get the right combination of hook material, floatability and length, you might have to buy one manufacturer's pole and another's hook.

Mooring equipment

A useful item is a mooring loop which is used with the special boathook. Make a loop (about 50 centimetres diameter) in a rope that is rigid enough to keep its shape. Then make two loops from strong string (just big enough to accept the special boathook) and tie them on to the large loop. You will find this extremely useful when you want to get a line on to a distant bollard (see Fig 3.4).

Fig 3.4 Mooring loop.

If there are no mooring bollards, you will need spikes and a hammer to drive them in. The type with a ring at the end can be driven in further and is more easily pulled out when you want to leave, using a bar inserted through the loop.

In later chapters, various mooring and locking techniques will be described.

Insert end of boathook
into string loops and pole
out until main loop is
over bollard.

Pull boathook carefully
back so that loop drops
down over bollard.

Fig 3.5 Using a mooring loop.

After reading them, you may want to add to your lines.

Anchors

You should fit a stern anchor. Sooner or later, you may need to lie just off a rocky bank and you daren't risk being turned by wind, tide or current into the navigable channel.

Rudder position indicator/emergency tiller

Various countries expect you to have some sort of emergency steering device, even if it is only an oar or something similar. That apart, a proper emergency tiller is something that every wheel-steered boat ought to carry, as the following story illustrates.

Shortly after we had bought our *vlet*, we were sliding past a dock in the dark when, without warning, a Royal Navy training vessel peeled off the quay and headed straight for us. We wound on full starboard lock and full throttle, whilst emitting a series of very short hoots to warn the Navy of impending collision! At that, the radio burst into life and a voice squeaked, 'We'll go green to green'. This time we wound on full port lock, closed the throttle, and the Navy passed with centimetres to spare, disappearing into the night and leaving us with a broken

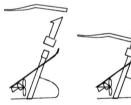

steering cable! An emergency tiller had come with the boat and, in under a minute, it was rigged. That is the only time it's been used in an emergency, but the incident did focus the mind on the need to 'Be Prepared'! In inland waterways we use part of the emergency tiller as a rudder position indicator (see Fig 3.6).

The parts of an emergency tiller.

Emergency tiller in use.

Used without handle, as rudder position indicator.

Fig 3.6 The emergency tiller.

Imagine that you have hurriedly entered a busy lock,

urged on by an insistent keeper, then are kept waiting whilst the lock is held for another barge. It could be quite a while before you finally release 'your' rope and go back to the helm, and by then you might have forgotten where the rudder was when you secured. You cannot afford just to move off and risk hitting another vessel, so you have to spin the wheel left, then right, to find the central position. That's a situation where, with barges looming closer behind, panic and shouting at each other tends to ensue! Using part of the emergency tiller as a rudder indicator means that you always know exactly which way the rudder is pointing.

Paraffin lamp

When moored alongside the bank at night, you must show a white light, visible all round, so we carry a paraffin lamp in case we have a power failure.

Tunnel light

This can double as a snooper scarer and, ideally, should have a swivelling mount. Buy the most powerful one you can afford.

Binoculars

This is a vital piece of equipment, which should always be to hand. If you wait to distinguish signs and general activity at locks and bridges with the naked eye, you could be in the wrong place for smooth passage.

Axe

Mount a very sharp one in the cockpit. It is always possible that a rope will snag in a lock and an axe will cut it more quickly than a knife.

Safety equipment

Fire extinguishers Safety equipment is already mandatory in most continental countries, and it is wise to conform. Suppose a fire started in your galley area and destroyed your boat whilst you were cruising France. One of your first visitors would be from the Comité de Surveillance, and he would not be impressed to find a 13 kilogram butane cylinder under the cooker, and just one fire extinguisher at the other end of the boat. His report might say, 'This boat was not safely fitted out and did not have adequate fire fighting equipment'. If this information reached your insurance company, it might prejudice your claim.

Near the engine bay you should have these extinguishers:
- Single-engine installations up to 200 hp, one household Type 21B.
- Single-engine installations above 200 hp, one household Type 34B.
- Twin-engine installations up to 400 hp, two household Type 21B.
- In addition, boats equipped with petrol engine installations exceeding 150 hp should have an inert gas extinguishing system.
- In all cases, an additional Type 21B extinguisher should be near the cooker. Depending on the boat's layout, it may be prudent to have additional extinguishers in other areas.

Fire blanket This is useful for minor fires and is very effective when clothing catches fire.

Lifejackets Allow one for each person, with a hydrostatic lift of at least 7.5 kilograms.

Lifebuoy One (minimum hydrostatic lift 7.5 kilograms) for boats up to 12 metres. Two (one at each end) for boats over 12 metres. Each should have a cord (of at least 10 metres) attached.

Dinghy

You'll find lots of waterways that are too small for your vessel. Brugge, for example, has a host of tiny canals, which can only be explored in a small boat. A dinghy, swung on davits, can also store grubby, smelly objects, like spare diesel cans. Ideally, it should have a small outboard. If you have a dinghy (and not much deck space), davits are essential in order to avoid tripping over the dinghy when you cross the deck in a hurry. Don't try towing – we tried it, on our first cruise, and the dinghy narrowly escaped destruction in the first lock.

Flags

You'll need your own ensign plus courtesy flags for those countries you intend to visit. (One tricolour, flown the right way or at right angles, can double for France and Holland.) Take a red distress flag, on a suitable pole. In Belgium, you need to fly a red flag with a white square in the middle at the bow when 'in commission'. (Make sure you have a suitable fitment.) This flag is not readily available from UK chandlers, but you can easily make one at home.

Spare fuel

One of the few things that will make a diesel engine stop is contaminated fuel. If possible, fit a reserve tank and keep at least 5 litres in a can.

First aid box

Cuts, bruises, burns from exhaust pipes, and scalds from dislodged kettles are the most common mishaps. Also take liberal supplies of mosquito repellant plus anti-histamines for anyone who is seriously affected by bites. In places where there may be sewage in the waterway, we use a Dettol solution to rinse our hands after handling ropes.

Generator

If your engine doesn't have hand-starting capability, a generator (with battery-charging facility) makes for peace of mind at out-of-the-way moorings. It need not be a super-silent and expensive leisure type. Our 2 kva site unit, with 10 amp charging, made by a small firm (*Exchange & Mart* advert), has given 12 years' reliable service for a fraction of the cost of its 'big name' equivalent.

Miscellaneous equipment

Trolley After a few kilometres, shopping gets very heavy so you need something more substantial than the 'wheels' used by cross-Channel beer hunters for haul-ing heavy objects (like 25 litres of diesel) along roughish canal paths, and it should have pneumatic tyres. Try dealers in secondhand machine tools and/or agricultural equipment.

Pieces of fine netting (used for net curtains) fastened over open hatches will keep out mosquitoes.

Strong adhesive-backed fabric tape (from agricultural machinery specialists) will secure netting and many other items – eg holding something in place whilst you motor to a chandlery for a new bracket.

A good waterproof torch, with spare bulbs and batteries (French supermarkets sell very cheap batteries).

A bailer.

At least one strong 7 litre bucket, with 2 metres of soft rope attached to the handle.

Portable horn operated by an aerosol container.

Thermos flask, or flasks, so that early wakers can have morning tea without rousing everyone.

Permanent fixtures

The things we've talked about so far could be termed loose items, but there are a few permanent fixtures to consider adding if they aren't already part of your boat's equipment:

Speed indicator (log)

Some owners rely on judging speed from the appearance of wash, waves breaking on the bank etc. However, radar traps are not unknown (several have been installed on UK rivers) so buying a log is better than risking a fine.

Radio

This is not needed on many UK waterways, but is a must at sea and when entering ports. Ones with a detachable, or additional handheld receiver have a big advantage, as the expensive bit can be bolted down below, out of sight.

Deck fittings

(a) (b)

Bitts and cleats The average boat has woefully small items, barely suitable for attaching the boat to a marina pontoon in still water. Decent-sized items are essen-tial for hassle-free lock passages, so

Fig 3.7 (a) These are suitable bitts. (b) These are unsuitable.

upgrade them if necessary (see Fig 3.7). Later, we'll describe our 'leapfrog' tech-nique for deep locks, which uses a centre bitt. If you haven't got one (or only have a small one), fit a large one. Angled bitts are a bonus when mooring at high quays.

Stanchions Narrow boats apart (and that's only because it would probably be impossible), stanchions and a wire, or a solid rail, must be fitted. Even strong

Fig 3.8 Stanchions reduce the risk of falling overboard.

swimmers could be sucked under if thrown overboard in a lock (see Fig 3.8).

Grab rails Fit grab rails to cabin tops and wheelhouse roofs. This is imperative on narrow boats, with outside walkways, where it is the only security against falling in. An additional rail running across the front roof gives added security on a narrow boat with a small foredeck.

Non-slip surfaces Any surfaces where you walk, or might walk, when mooring, locking etc should have a non-slip surface or 'stepping stones' (see Fig 3.9). Our decks are painted with non-slip paint, and we have also painted a section of the wheelhouse roof with non-slip paint – useful when we want to work on the mast. On the coachroof, we have stuck patches of Treadmaster (cheap offcuts) for occasions when we need to jump down from a high quay.

Fig 3.9 Use non-slip paints or patches on decks etc.

Gas bottles

Most European waterway authorities already insist that gas bottles (except small ones, designed to bolt directly to lights etc) should be kept outside accommodation areas, in a well-ventilated place. In any case, even when this is not compulsory, it is common sense to minimise the risk of gas accumulating in the bilges. The simplest solution is to strap bottles on deck (away from hatches and other openings into the boat), as this will enable you to use cheaper, household bottles. (On the Continent you'll need a different regulator, available from hypermarkets.) If you want to stick to small bottles, and have an open cockpit, you may be able to modify a cockpit locker, provided it is above the waterline and made of a suitable material (see Fig 3.11).

In some countries, hypermarket filling stations sell gas in big bottles, and inside you'll find the smaller camping type. In rural areas (not on mains gas) you'll find other stockists of large bottles.

Canopy

Continental Europe is often very much hotter than the UK. Towels, bedding etc hung over cabin window and skylights help to keep cabins cool, but you can't really leave them there whilst you go off for the day. A demountable canopy will ensure that you come back to a cooler interior (see Fig 3.10).

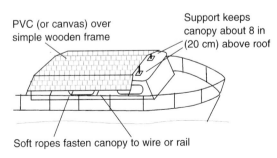

PVC (or canvas) over simple wooden frame

Support keeps canopy about 8 in (20 cm) above roof

Soft ropes fasten canopy to wire or rail

Fig 3.10 Keep it cool.

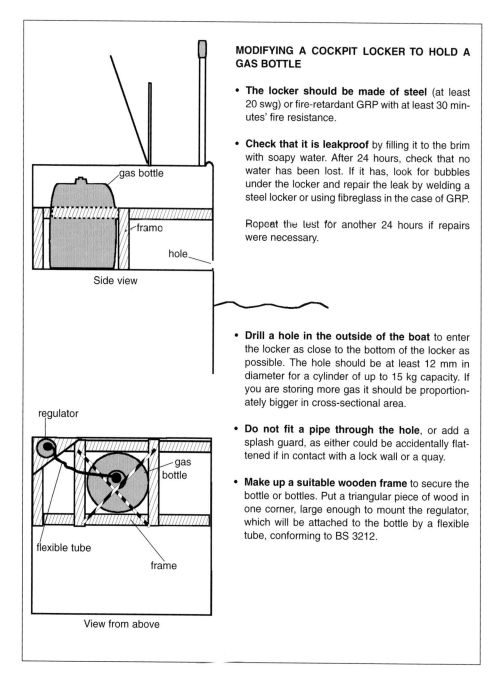

MODIFYING A COCKPIT LOCKER TO HOLD A GAS BOTTLE

- **The locker should be made of steel** (at least 20 swg) or fire-retardant GRP with at least 30 minutes' fire resistance.

- **Check that it is leakproof** by filling it to the brim with soapy water. After 24 hours, check that no water has been lost. If it has, look for bubbles under the locker and repair the leak by welding a steel locker or using fibreglass in the case of GRP.

  Repeat the test for another 24 hours if repairs were necessary.

- **Drill a hole in the outside of the boat** to enter the locker as close to the bottom of the locker as possible. The hole should be at least 12 mm in diameter for a cylinder of up to 15 kg capacity. If you are storing more gas it should be proportionately bigger in cross-sectional area.

- **Do not fit a pipe through the hole,** or add a splash guard, as either could be accidentally flattened if in contact with a lock wall or a quay.

- **Make up a suitable wooden frame** to secure the bottle or bottles. Put a triangular piece of wood in one corner, large enough to mount the regulator, which will be attached to the bottle by a flexible tube, conforming to BS 3212.

Fig 3.11 Gas locker.

Fridge

This is useful for keeping food and drink cool in hot weather. We use the type that runs from a battery when we are under way and is then switched to gas when we moor. Wire it through the starter switch, so it goes off when the engine isn't running, or you could wake up to a flat battery by forgetting to change over. (If you don't have a fridge put the beer in the bilges when on the move, and hang it over the side in a fishing net when moored.)

Wiring tip

Whether your electrical system can operate tele-visions, fridges, microwaves etc will largely be dependent on the depth of your pocket. However, you can improve most basic systems quite cheaply; eg if you put fuse blocks, terminals etc into modern plastic household boxes (Hagar, Legrand, etc), they are less likely to 'fur up' due to atmospheric corro-sion. Running the wiring through a flexible conduit will protect it from accidental damage (see Fig 3.12).

Fig 3.12 Household electrical box and flexible conduit.

Pre-cruise checks

One difference between the cruising that you've done to date, and that which you might do on inland waterways, could be the number of hours of continuous running. When leisurely hopping from one pleasant mooring place to another, you won't do anything unusual in hours per day, but when aiming to reach a new cruising ground quickly, matters can be very different – especially when the unexpected happens.

On one voyage, we planned to cruise eight hours per day, but late on the third day we suddenly found ourselves surrounded by suds, like the outpouring of some giant washing machine. Next the echo sounder squawked and our propeller churned up vast quantities of mud. It turned out that a Belgian river had burst its bank, devastated a chemical storage area, and swept mud and debris into the French canal we were using as a short cut. By the time we had extricated ourselves and found a night's resting place, we had travelled 112 kilometres and been motoring for 14 hours. The moral of the story is that prolonged running creates heat build-up in the engine bay, and when mechanical components get hot any weakness will show up.

Checking your boat over is an excellent way of learning all about it, as well as a good way of ensuring that nothing goes wrong. At the same time as doing your checks, you can make a list of spares to take with you. You may also glean useful information during the checkover. For example, few people know the precise position of the echo sounder probe, relative to the lowest part of the boat. It scarcely matters at sea, but a few centimetres can be very important when you're creeping towards a bank, or trying to get up a delightful shallow creek. It's also important to know your air draft; it could save you having to open certain bridges.

Fuel system

On peaceful rivers and flat calm seas, fuel filter problems are rare. They start when boats get bounced around and sediment is swirled up, or rust particles become dislodged from inner surfaces. Removing your tanks and having them cleaned will eliminate this problem. (Try your local car radiator repair specialist.)

Plastic tanks are not a guarantee against filter problems, because old diesel can form a glutinous deposit; this hardens where not immersed, then flakes off when the boat is bounced about. Nor will picking a calm day for a sea passage necessarily ensure that anything undesirable stays on the tank sides or below the fuel pick-up. In the Channel, dozens of up-and-down ship movements, plus crossing ferries and hovercraft, make plenty of wash!

Cooling system

Hoses that look OK *whilst undisturbed* can in fact be near to failure. Squeeze each one and replace any that show cracks or are not pliable. You can buy convoluted hose (motor and lorry factors) that, according to where you cut, fits various pipe sizes; take a length with you. Slightly unscrew hose securing clips (to make sure they aren't seized) and retighten. Use a small hacksaw to cut through any you can't undo. (Don't cut the hose as well!) Replace these, plus any rusty ones. Screws on clips that were installed during engine assembly may be almost inaccessible with the engine in the boat; reposition these.

Check fan belt adjustments; they must not be slack, but there should be 'give' when you press between pulleys. Take spares with you.

The best filters can let particles through that eventually abrade rubber water pump impellers. If your pump's impeller is replaceable, take a spare.

The most common cooling system draws in sea, river or canal water through a filter, then pumps it round the engine. Dismantle your filter, or filters, and check the condition. There should be no rips, nor signs of impending collapse, in bronze gauze types. Renew any that are not in good condition and take a spare, plus several extra sealing rings.

A sealed engine cooling system in a boat is similar to the one in your car, and should be filled with an appropriate antifreeze solution. Hot water from the engine is pumped through fins, or pipes, in bilge keels, then cooled water returns to the engine. This system eliminates possible engine overheating due to filter blockage, but even boats with sealed engine cooling systems may have a raw water system for oil and exhaust cooling. Check the condition of this filter and take spare rings. Filters must be checked daily and rubber sealing rings can distort after being refitted a number of times. If appropriate, take a spare impeller for the pump in the oil cooling system.

Drawing debris into a water filter is inevitable and, in reedy rivers and tree-lined canals, we sometimes have to clean them more often than once a day. You should keep regular checks on water outlet to ensure that flow is normal, but on inland waterways it's easy to get distracted by the sight of yet another castle, and forget about checking outflow or gauges. So, as well as your engine temperature gauge, you should have some additional warning of impending overheating for each system. Red lights, which illuminate if the temperature goes higher than 10 degrees above the norm, are easy to fit and quickly attract attention. An audible warning is even better.

Engine/gearbox lubrication systems
Check all unions, by releasing slightly and retightening. Change oil and filters, in both systems, unless you've recently had a service. Check filters for leaks and take spare filter rings.

Fuel pumps and filters
Your fuel supply pump may have an internal filter gauze. Remove and clean it, and renew it if it has any holes. Take spare copper, or fibre, washers (whichever is fitted). You may have a remote filter/water trap; if so, drain and clean this and, again, take a spare sealing ring.

Engine bay
Thoroughly clean the engine bay using a proprietary cleaner from a motor factor. Heat gradually builds up, the longer you go on running, and a hot oily engine bay gives off fumes. At best these fumes smell unpleasant, and at worst they could make someone feel seasick. Also, if a leak starts it will be more obvious in a clean engine bay. Secondly, if your engine bay is oily, when you pump the bilges you will be putting out an oily mixture. Anti-pollution rules are getting stricter, and leaving a slick behind could mean a fine.

Engine mountings
Your engine will probably be fitted with bonded rubber mountings; examine them for signs of perishing and damage. Like everything else, the mountings will get hot on a long run and could eventually fail if repeatedly jolted. The chances of weak mountings failing is accentuated in canals because bumping solid objects, like lock walls, is a more regular occurrence.

Engine starting
Poor diesel engine starting is usually down to glow plugs that don't glow, or dirty/worn injectors. If you've been having problems, first check that the glow plugs are receiving a supply of current. If they are, have them tested and renew if necessary. If the plugs are OK, suspect the injectors. In most towns there will be a diesel specialist (see *Yellow Pages*) who can clean them and check for wear.

When cruising carry an aerosol of engine starting spray. Worn injectors can also mean unburned fuel dripping from your exhaust, or excessive smoke, which would make you very unpopular with the authorities of certain countries.

Stern gland

Stern glands are often located in an inaccessible place, and no one wants to start each day grovelling in the bilges with a sticky grease gun. If your stern gland needs regular greasing, a remote greasing system is a worthwhile feature, and you can make one yourself. Secondhand machine tool dealers usually have a few scrap machines and this is where to look for a suitable unit.

Mount it in a locker, or other convenient place, where people can't brush against it. Then (using string) measure the route of a pipe from the remote unit to the stern gland grease nipple. Obviously you'll have to drill some access holes. Take string, greaser and nipple to a firm that specialises in making up hydraulic pipes (a specialist in hydraulics, diesel equipment, or even a trade motor factor). They will supply a connecting pipe (appropriate to the pressure of the grease), either in a flexible material or the type of rigid material that is easily bent without kinking. When mounting, remember to fit grommets at access holes and retain the pipe with several clips.

Steering

Check for wear in any joints and verify that attachment points are secure.

Lights

Check that exterior and interior lights are working and take spare bulbs.

Gas system

Check that unions are tight and that pipes that pass through bulkheads are protected by grommets.

External fittings

The first fixed bridge on the Canal de Calais is low enough to sweep away most radio aerials. Discovering that the aerial securing bolts are seized when you're in sight of that bridge is hardly an ideal situation, so your pre-cruise preparations should include checking fixings on any 'above wheelhouse' fittings that might need to come down. Undo and retighten each fixing, greasing where appropriate.

Tools

When you have finished checking the boat, your tool box should contain the spanners etc you may need on the voyage. Add things like insulating tape, spare electrical wire, mole grips, pliers.

Things to know, before you go

In this chapter we're going to cover the regulatory requirements of various countries, as well as answering some other frequently asked questions.

Do I need a Certificate of Competence?

Since the first edition was written, the problem concerning the lack of a recognised UK International Certificate of Competence has been resolved. After the Maritime & Coastguard Agency had attended meetings of the United Nations Principal Working Party on Inland Transport, it was agreed that a UK ICC, with inland waterway endorsement, would only be issued after the applicant had passed a written test proving knowledge of CEVNI.

This certificate is not required in most countries for small craft, though it isn't a bad idea to have one anyway; in the event of an accident, it shows a degree of competence which could stand you in good stead.

France The certificate is required in France, where it is valid for boats up to 15 metres long. If your boat is longer then the only way to be legal on the French waterways is to obtain a French Péniche de Plaisance certificate. This is not difficult to obtain; if you are competent enough to go through the canals with your 15+ metre boat, you are competent enough to pass the practical test, which involves carrying out simple manoeuvres including going through a lock.

The theoretical test involves knowing CEVNI. Normally it is conducted in French, but as it is largely pictorial, this shouldn't be a huge problem and we do know of several people who have passed without knowing much French. If your knowledge of the language is nil, we have been assured that the Douai branch of the French Service de Navigation, which covers the channel ports, will arrange for an interpreter at your expense.

Holland You only require a certificate of competence if your boat is over 15 metres long, or capable of more than 20 kph under engine. For boats in this category an ICC with inland endorsement is sufficient for canals, rivers and estuaries. To clear up any possible confusion about other certificates; for the Schelde, Waddenzee, IJsselmeer, Eems and Dollard it is not necessary to have an ICC if you hold a Yachtmaster or Coastal Skipper qualification.

Germany Regulations include a 'guest rule' which permits those who are not resident in Germany to use a vessel on German waterways for up to a year. The conditions are that the vessel's displacement must be under 20 cubic metres.

However, there is one exception; the river Rhine, which is not governed by the German authorities, but by the Rhine Commission. This is Europe's busiest commercial waterway carrying 300 million tons of freight every year, and the Commission has introduced a Rhine Sports Patent which is required to legally navigate on the river. The Patent is issued for specific stretches, and among other requirements, obtaining it requires proof of a number of passages on that stretch. It is therefore, virtually impossible for someone who is not a resident in that particular area to obtain the qualification. The only way for most non-resident pleasure craft owners to legally navigate on the Rhine today is to take a qualified person with them.

In general, other European countries only require visitors to have the certificate required in their own country, which in the case of the UK is none.

Although there is no obligation to have passed any test before you drive a boat in UK waters, you can take a one or two day Royal Yachting Association inland cruising course. When you have successfully completed it, you receive the RYA Inland Waterway Helmsman's Certificate. The course assumes no previous knowledge of boating so, as well as getting supervised practice in boat handling, anyone taking it will receive instruction on many subjects, such as tying knots, man overboard techniques and boat safety.

We recommend that everyone about to embark on cruising the inland waterways takes the RYA course and the important thing is to choose the right examination centre, so that you get maximum benefit from what you are being taught. If you intend to go narrow boat cruising, choose a centre on a narrow canal, even if you will mainly be using broad ones. That way you will have practised the most difficult narrow boating techniques under instruction, and when you are on your own, coping on broad waterways will be relatively easy.

Do countries charge for use of the inland waterways?

France In France, you pay a 'Péage Plaisance' on waterways controlled by Voies Navigables de France. 2003 rates (Euros) are:

	Yearly rate	Leisure rate	Holiday rate
Up to 12 m²	74.00	43.00	16.00
12 m² to 25 m²	106.00	76.00	33.00
25 m² to 40 m²	213.00	134.00	49.00
40 m² to 60 m²	344.00	209.00	65.00
over 60 m²	426.00	259.00	82.00

Note that rates are per square metre, not per metre length. That is length times beam, as given in the registration document. There is 10 percent discount for payment before March 20th, but remember that the fee is not refundable. Leisure rate allows small craft to cruise for 30 days, which need not be consecutive. Holiday rate is valid for 16 consecutive days which must be specified when purchasing.

When applying, supply the following information:

- Boat's name
- Owner's name and address
- Length/beam measurements
- Registration number. If possible, enclose photocopy of the registration document.

Include an addressed envelope and international reply coupon if applying by post. Send a cheque (in Euros), or make a bank transfer to VNF Bethune. Bank Code 10071. Cashiers Code 62100. Account number 10003010, key 14. Give details in application letter.

French waterways not under VNF control are marked on an overall map, available free from VNF. Local tourist boards will supply details of charges (if any).

In France there are just a few cases where payment is required for specialised services (eg boat lifts and tunnel tows). Often there is a free, but usually slower, alternative.

Virtually everywhere on the French canals, mooring alongside the bank or at town quays is free. Generally, town quays have no special facilities for pleasure craft, but there are exceptions. France, expecially in the north, excels at providing pontoons marked 'Halte Fluviale' (simple pontoon) or 'Relais Fluviale' (some facilities, often being continually improved upon) where you can also moor without charge. At a 'Base Fluviale' (marina) you pay. Often there is a standard extra charge for electricity, which is not related to the amount you use and can therefore be disproportionately expensive. Sometimes showers are extra.

Holland There is no general fee for the use of Dutch waterways, but on many of Holland's more picturesque canals (throughout Friesland and on the Vecht, for example) a clog is swung down at every lifting bridge. Dutch regulations stipulate that payment should only be made when an official sign 'Brugge Geld' is displayed. However, we have not met anyone who has dared to refuse unauthorised demands for fear of encountering delays.

Many Dutch towns have small harbours (called Passentenhaven), or quays, where those passing through can moor free for specified periods. This can vary from a few hours for shopping to 48 hours. Outside the busiest times, some towns will allow you to stay longer than the specified period (ask at the Town Hall).

Free Dutch country moorings are not easy to find for a number of reasons:

extensive reed beds, high steeply sloping canal banks, quays reserved for commercial vessels etc. The West Overijssel is an exception to this rule – many beautiful moorings have been set up, where you are invited to remain for up to 48 hours. In Friesland, it is very difficult to find a free mooring. Practically every town charges for use of its quay and the banks surrounding the town. However, charges are not expensive, and there are often excellent shower/toilet blocks at the quays.

Electricity is often available, at both free and paying moorings from a metered supply, and in many cases you will also have to feed a slot if you want to put water in your tanks.

Dutch marina prices are not expensive; electricity is usually extra – by coin operated meter – but water and showers are usually included in the overall charge.

United Kingdom The UK's system of charges is complex, because the waterways are not administered by a single authority and there are many options – short stay, use of whole (or part) of a region, use with (or without) lock passage etc. Also, some authorities charge by metre length of boat and others by the square metre (ie. length multiplied by beam). It would take several pages to list all options and we think the space can be better used to supply harder-to-get information. The authority controlling waterways in your planned cruising area will send a list of charges.

Most UK locks etc are free, but there are exceptions.

In the UK, you can often find country moorings permitting a free stay of a specified period, but most town/village moorings charge. Marina prices vary according to facilities. You can moor free on the towpath side of most British Waterways canals (provided you are not a hindrance to passing boats). The non-towpath side of a canal and both banks of a river will probably be private property, so ask permission before mooring.

Belgium Belgian waterways are controlled by two authorities, Flanders (Flemish speaking area nearest to UK) and Wallonie (French speaking area). Cruising Wallonie is inexpensive and informal, you simply pay a small fee at the first lock you come to and may be asked to show your receipt at locks en route. The fee covers you for a considerable distance, but you may be required to pay again depending on your route.

In Flanders you are required to display a *vignette* on the starboard side of the boat. This can be purchased on arrival in Belgium at many locks and port offices, or you can write to Dienst voor de Scheepvaart, Havenstraat 44, 3500 Hasselt, Belgium, who will also send you an information pack, maps etc.

In Belgium, marina prices vary considerably, since some are very much more sophisticated than others, but there are plenty of free quay and bankside moorings.

Germany In general you don't have to pay canal dues in Germany but there are a few exceptions. eg the Kiel canal.

Some major German rivers (eg the Moselle) have free pleasure boat locks (next to commercial ones) operating in the summer months. At other times you may have to pay to use the commercial lock.

You can find free quays and pontoons but marina moorings are easier to locate and not expensive.

Scandinavia In Scandinavia, there may be permit charges for the use of a canal (eg the Saimaa canal) or you may be charged a lock fee. Sometimes the overall fee includes marina moorings, so you need to check with the waterway you plan to travel. That said, lock fees can make up a considerable part of Scandinavian holiday expenses, but don't let that put you off a Scandinavian cruise, especially in a trailer boat; on many canals you can cruise vast expanses without using any locks.

Many Scandinavian lifting bridges are self operated and free; when bridge charges are made they are usually small.

In both Norway and Sweden, everyone has the right of access to private land (other than cultivated fields and the land immediately around a dwelling). This not only means that you can moor free anywhere but that you can pick berries, mushrooms etc. There are also free moorings at certain town quays and many towns provide free pontoon moorings for visitors.

Note that, even in countries which do not normally charge for lock use, you may have to pay at sea locks leading to canals. There is no hard and fast rule about which ports charge and which do not.

I've heard I need a Shengen visa. What does this mean?

The name 'Schengen' originates from a small town in Luxembourg. In March 1995, seven EU countries signed a treaty to end internal border checkpoints and control and more have joined the treaty over the past years. At present there are 15 Schengen countries: Austria, Belgium, Denmark, Finland, France, Germany, Iceland, Italy, Greece, Luxembourg, Netherlands, Norway, Portugal, Spain and Sweden. All except Norway and Iceland are European Union members.

As you can see, the UK is not a Schengen country. A few years back this didn't much matter but, with heightened security concerns this no longer applies and UK residents need to have a Schengen visa before crossing the Channel. For further information read Chapter 5 on information for US visitors.

Are inland waterways open all year round?

Every effort is made to keep Europe's main commercial waterways open, but ice, flooding, drought, silting, lock/bridge failure and burst banks can bring traffic to an unexpected halt. Details of problems (and closures for maintenance) are posted at locks, in trade magazines such as Holland's *De Scheepvartkrant* and some leisure boating magazines. Some countries have planned periods when canals are closed for repairs.

United Kingdom In the UK, details of planned closures can be obtained from the relevant navigation authority. Details of unexpected British Waterways closures are given on recorded telephone messages.

France The French *Liste des chomages*, obtainable from Voies Navigables de France, covers closures for reasons of maintenance, repair or major reconstruction and is accompanied by a map. Closures may be for as little as a day, or for several months.

For geographical and climatic reasons, certain French waterways are more affected by drought than those in other continental regions. Before leaving home, consult Voies Navigables de France's website to find out about conditions in your chosen area. Keep a special lookout at locks for notices headed *Avis de Batellerie*.

The Canal du Midi is used for irrigation purposes in summer, so sailors using this as a route to the Med need to be especially careful if their yacht is close to the maximum authorised draught.

Scandinavia In the north of mainland Europe, winter temperatures tend to be lower than on the corresponding UK latitude, so many non-commercial waterways will be closed in winter. Also, many Scandinavian canals have insufficient tourist traffic to justify continued employment of lock keepers, so they close around the end of August. If you are planning to go north other than in summer, check with the tourist boards.

Can I cruise at any time of the day and night?
The majority of waterways are not suitable for night/poor visibility navigation. Signs are not illuminated, you cannot see the banks (or any hazards near them) and the result of falling overboard in the dark could be disastrous.

Some major through routes are equipped with lights, radar reflectors etc, so that commercial traffic can continue 24 hours a day. Even so, we would not recommend that you join in. Masters of huge commercial vessels do not expect to meet tiny boats at night or in fog, and your near-insignificant radar blip could be masked by a larger vessel. In any case, it is unlikely that your boat will have the right type of radar set, or that you will have the appropriate qualification. Another danger of night travel is the increased likelihood of fog building up over the waterway. In any case, inland waterway cruising is all about seeing places, and hurtling down the Lek, for example, on a night tide is scarcely the way to get maximum pleasure from this beautiful river.

In most countries (except on major international routes) operators of manned locks/bridges work specific hours. In the UK you are sometimes allowed to operate these locks yourself if the operator has gone home.

Belgium Belgium imposes both lock and navigating hours, which vary throughout the year. In July, for example, most locks are open from around 6 am to 7.30 pm, whilst navigation hours are from 4.30 am to 9.30 pm. Certain individual locks, bridges and/or canals have specific opening (or non-opening) times. For example, many lifting bridges are not opened for canal traffic at times when many people are travelling to and from work. Wallonian Belgian locks and bridges do not open on Sundays and bank holidays; many Flemish ones, in popular tourist areas, do open for pleasure craft on at least part of Sunday and bank holidays, hence the disparity between canal permit charges in the two regions. Details of the Flemish timetable are available from the Hasselt address in Appendix B.

Scandinavia In Scandinavia, locks tend to close early and open late (regional and seasonal variations). However, as the majority of inland waterways consist of vast lakes linked by short canals, you can still explore a maze of creeks and islets during the long summer daylight.

What insurance cover do I need for the boat?

Amazingly, some countries don't insist that you have any; in others, the level of obligatory third party insurance is quite high. In truth, you would be foolish not to have insurance. Canal travelling is not normally a high-risk pursuit, but if your boat happened to catch fire near a tanker barge the result could be spectacular, to say the least. Whether third party insurance had been obligatory or not, the barge's insurers would almost certainly endeavour to recoup a part of their enormous loss from you. Write to your insurance company, tell them where you intend to cruise, and ask what level of insurance they recommend. At the same time, you can also ask whether you need insurance for push bikes. Be sure to get their reply in writing and check that your policy covers you for accidentally polluting the waterways with oily mixtures. In addition to a fine, you might also be liable for a clean-up job if you seriously polluted certain areas.

Carry a copy of your insurance certificate with you. In some countries this is obligatory, in the rest prudent.

What documents should I have on board?

You must have on board:
- Your boat's Certificate of Registry.
- A ship's log.
- The appropriate navigating regulations (unless the authorities of the waterway concerned have waived that requirement for small pleasure craft).

On most British Waterways you need a Safety Certificate. Exceptions about this are made for temporary visitors, who may have to undergo an inspection prior to entering the waterway, but check with the authorities before setting off for a new area.

Most countries require you to carry a copy of the *International Regulations For The Prevention Of Collisions At Sea* and copies of the inland waterway regulations. In most cases, *The RYA Book of EuroRegs for Inland Waterways* (Adlard Coles Nautical) will be accepted as a pleasure craft users version of CEVNI, but you may also need copies of certain additional local regulations, eg Rhine rules if you are travelling that river and the tributaries and canals which come under the jurisdiction of the Rhine Commission.

Holland requires any boat visiting its waters to carry copies of the *Binnenvaartpolitiereglement*. This is only published in Dutch but the most easily understood version can be obtained from NUMIJ, Postbus 4, 2300 Leiden.

Many countries expect you to have a copy of your Certificate of Insurance on board.

Are there any rules about the equipment I must have on the boat?

In most countries boats belonging to that country's residents have to undergo a safety inspection. During the inspection, the equipment is checked to make sure that it conforms to what the particular country regards as essential. We've already mentioned that if a vessel were involved in an accident, a foreign official or loss adjuster might apply his country's rules to a UK registered ship, and if it did not conform, might say that it was not adequately equipped.

There is a simple precaution you should take, which will ensure that in the event of an accident or fire your insurance company would not be able to say that you were inadequately equipped. Send them a copy of your boat's equipment and a letter saying 'I intend to cruise the inland waterways of these countries... Do you consider the equipment on the attached list to be adequate?' Take their written reply with you.

In some places, for example Finland's Saimaa canal, your boat undergoes an inspection prior to transit.

Do I need a radio on board?

Small craft are not normally required to have a radio, but those that are installed must conform to the requirements of the appropriate authorities. If you do have a radio, you must obtain a licence from Ships Radio Licensing (see Appendix B), and someone on board must have an Operator's Certificate, obtained by passing an RYA examination. You must carry both the VHF licence and the VHF Operator's Certificate on board.

You must not use your radio for unauthorised communication; you should listen in on the channel prescribed by the authorities. On the Rhine, vessels on passage normally listen, simultaneously, on boat-to-boat and information frequencies. Also on the Rhine, small craft need a radio if they intend to navigate by radar. Other craft must have a set in good order that can receive and send on boat-to-boat, boat-to-port and information frequencies, and that conforms to requirements in *Guide de Radiotéléphonie pour la Navigation Rhénane*. The boat's papers must include this Guide (obtainable from the Rhine Commission) plus a radio installation licence and a crew member's certificate of competence in radio telephony.

We would strongly recommend that anyone intending to cruise to the Continent installs a radio and obtains the necessary qualification. Calais Port controllers say that the situation they dread is a ferry leaving, another arriving and a small non-radio boat bobbing about at the harbour entrance. Controllers at other busy ports express similar sentiments.

Before you buy a radio, make sure that it has the appropriate channels for canal use, in addition to those needed for port entries. The canal channels that are in most frequent use are Boat to Boat 10, 13, 73 and 77; Boat to Port Authority 11, 12, 13 and 14; Navigation Information 18, 20, 22, 78, 79, 80, 81 and 82 (the majority of locks are on 18, 20 and 22).

Holland has introduced a requirement for radios to be fitted with Automatic Calling Identification. If your radio does not have this you will be considered to be a non-radio vessel and should not transmit. Also, radios used on Dutch inland waterways should have a capability of being able to transmit at only ? watt.

Can I use radar on inland waterways?

Radar sets used on waterways where radar navigation is permitted must be suitable for inland waterway use and approved by specified countries, eg for the Rhine, sets must be approved by Belgium, or one of the countries bordering the river.

Vessels must have all necessary equipment (specified by the appropriate authorities) to navigate by radar, under conditions where this would otherwise make navigation impossible. One person fully conversant with radar navigation must always be in the wheelhouse (on the Rhine, that person must hold a Diploma, issued, after a test, by the Rhine Commission, in Strasbourg). A second person – sufficiently conversant to take over if necessary – must also be in the wheelhouse, or able to be called to the wheelhouse. On the Rhine, the second person must remain in the wheelhouse, unless the vessel concerned has a Rhine Surveillance Certificate, permitting radar navigation by one person.

In other words, it is highly unlikely that the radar fitted on your yacht will be suitable for inland navigation and equally unlikely that you will be qualified to use it.

What do I need to use for sound signals?

Sound signals (other than bells) are normally given by mechanically operated devices in high unobstructed positions. In most countries, small craft (not navigating by radar) may use a horn or trumpet. CEVNI requires countries that

Lock fees can make up a substantial part of Scandinavian cruising costs, but the scenery makes it worthwhile.

insist that small craft have a mechanically operated sound signalling device to exempt those coming from countries that do not.

If you are purchasing a sound signalling device (fixed or portable), this is the specification to ask for: operating frequency above 350 Hz; weighted sound pressure between 100 and 125 DB(A) (measured by sonometers IEC179 or 123, 1 metre in front of horn and as far as possible from sound reflecting material). Ask the supplier where the device should be mounted in order to avoid affecting the helmsman's hearing. (Weighted sound pressure, near his head, should not exceed 70DB(A).)

Will my electricity and gas fittings be OK abroad?

You will not be able to plug into many continental marina supplies with a UK plug on the end of your lead. You can buy converters in the UK or stop at a supermarket on the Continent and get the right plug.

Continental gas regulators are also different and can be purchased in super-markets, where you can also obtain bottles and refills.

Where do I dispose of waste water and sewage?

In the UK, a sea toilet outlet must be sealed before you enter inland waterways. There are severe penalties for unsealing and using it, and for throwing the contents of a Porta Potti in the canal.

Elsewhere, authorities are usually more concerned about the effects of oily pollutants, although theoretically, in many continental countries you are supposed to have holding tanks on inland waterways. In practice, there is often nowhere to empty them. This is a problem even for large commercial vessels. For example, many Danube barges have on board plants to handle sewage, so points to empty tanks are not required, creating difficulties for transiting western vessels.

In Switzerland, you must not even empty your sink water into inland waterways and lakes, and in Scandinavia, only someone utterly insensible would pollute the crystal clear lakes. In many cases, these are so pure that people fill their boat tanks directly from them.

We carry a Porta Potti which lives in the aft cabin during the day and is put in the hooded cockpit at night. This means that we are legal everywhere, and those sleeping in the aft cabin do not disturb those in the front if they need to use the toilet in the night.

How do I dispose of rubbish if I'm not staying in a marina?

On commercial waterways, locks and quays have rubbish disposal points – often divided into bins for plastic, glass and other waste – and increasingly, there are skips in supermarket carparks across the Continent.

At some popular moorings (eg Brugge), a van calls each day to collect the boat's rubbish. In such places, noone minds if you leave a bag against a tree, but you will meet disapproval in Scandinavia if you leave a sealed bin bag beside a full skip.

With the advent of European Directives on waste disposal, stuffing anything and everything – from your empty beer bottles to old paint tins – into a dustbin is no longer acceptable. If in doubt, ask someone.

Will I be able to get spare parts if I need them?

Contact the manufacturers of your engine, gearbox, electrical equipment and anything else vital to continued cruising, for a list of stockists in the area/country you intend to visit. If your engine is a marine version of a car/lorry engine, try the agent for the road-going version first, rather than a marine specialist. There are two reasons: firstly, anything with 'marine' attached to its name tends to be more expensive; secondly, agents for commercial vehicles, which must get back on the road quickly, are geared up for quick service. We had an example of this in Holland when our Daf suddenly started racing, and belching out clouds of white smoke. At 5 pm we went to the local Daf lorry distributor and said, 'Can you get us a governor diaphragm for our DD575?' At 8.30 am the next day, we were fitting it. That's pretty impressive when you consider that the engine had just celebrated its 28th birthday! Of course, on the Continent, barges are just as much part of the commercial world as lorries are, so a specialist in barges would undoubtedly have got our diaphragm just as quickly.

What maps, books etc should I have?

You will need the appropriate charts, tide tables and tidal stream tables and pilots for any sea/estuary on your route.

United Kingdom For the UK, Nicholson's series of four Ordnance Survey Guides to the Waterways (South, Central, North, River Thames and Broads & Fens) are very detailed and the text provides a lot of navigational and tourist information.

France Our favourite French maps are the Navicarte series, which also covers certain Belgian regions (eg the Meuse). The text is in three languages (including English) and the approach to locks, bridges etc are photographed from a 'boat's eye' view, with arrows indicating where you need to aim for.

The regional councils of France's Nord-Pas de Calais and western Belgium have produced a superb 270 page full colour book of navigation maps, with 250 pictures of interesting sights. It is called the Tourist Navigation Guide and is available in English, as well as French, Dutch & German, from Westtoer apb (see Appendix B).

Holland Most largish Dutch towns have a Royal Dutch Touring Club (ANWB) shop where you can buy canal/river maps. ANWB maps are clear, provide a lot of useful information and are fine for canal and river passages. The folded type tear easily, so put sellotape on the seams before you use them. For estuaries and large meers like those in Zeeland and the IJsselmeer, we would only buy the official *Hydrografische Kaarts*, which are available (with updating service) in the UK from Kelvin Hughes (see Appendix B).

Germany Our favourite source of German maps is Haus Rhein (see Appendix B). They will send you a catalogue on request.

Scandinavia The controlling bodies of most Scandinavian canals excel at publishing maps which, in addition to being an essential navigational aid, give a wealth of useful information ranging from tourist sites to where to find a dentist. You have to pay for them but they are worth every penny. The Scandinavian Tourist Offices will supply local addresses.

What if we need a doctor?

Before you leave the UK, get form E111 which entitles you to free medical treatment in countries with a reciprocal arrangement with the UK. However, it's usually a case of 'pay now, claim back later'. The exception is Sweden/Norway, where you only pay the contribution a local would pay and claim that back. In France, a standard consultation fee is not expensive and you can consult a *médecin specialisé* (a sort of cross between a specialist and a GP) for very little more. In Holland, Germany and Switzerland, doctors' fees can be alarming – we go direct to chemists for advice on deep cuts, burns etc. (You can even get your blood pressure checked at many continental chemists!) To guarantee reimbursement in full, choose a doctor/dentist who is *conventioné* (a practitioner who charges government-approved rates).

As a British citizen, if you are admitted to a continental hospital, fees will normally be claimed directly from the NHS, on production of form E111.

Can I use my Visa or Access card to get foreign currency, pay marina bills, buy food, get fuel for the boat, pay in restaurants etc?

Make sure that you have an international version of your credit card, as few overseas cashpoints accept other versions. Many Belgian/Dutch cashpoints (especially when outside tourist areas) only accept cards issued by the country's banks. In Belgium, you can obtain cash, with your cards, at most banks and international railway stations. Holland is similar and there is an organisation called GWK where you can obtain cash with your card. They have branches in many towns and are usually open late. At tourist border towns (eg Maastricht), avoid the 'change shops'; instead, go to a bank or GWK for the best rates.

In most countries, supermarkets take Visa/Access (sometimes a minimum purchase is specified). Small rural *auberges* (inns) may not accept cards, but will often take Eurocheques. Most marinas will expect cash.

In Scandinavia, you can use your card in towns, but elks and eagles and cashpoints and credit cards don't go together, so cash is best in rural areas.

Wherever you go, carry a reserve in travellers' cheques, including some small denominations, and a book of Eurocheques.

Will I have problems if I can't speak the language?

Even if you can't speak a word you will get by, because instructions are likely to be prefaced by 'Yacht', 'Sport Boat', or something that sounds like that. It doesn't usually take great linguistic ability to guess the rest. That said, your cruising days will be enriched if you can communicate with the locals. We feel most at home in France (where we are sufficiently fluent for the conversations one tends to have over a few jars in the cockpit) and in Sweden/Norway, where it is hard to find someone who does not speak near-perfect English.

We rate Longman's 'Survive In' series top for learning enough to simplify buying bread/meat/vegetables, getting directions to the bank/post office/restaurant, explaining that you've lost your passport/purse/child and asking 'What time does it [the lock, bridge, pub] open?' The advantage of this series is that you don't need to read a book at the same time as you listen to the tape. For a more advanced vocabulary, try Hugo's 'In Three Months' series. For technical vocabulary, the *Yachtsman's 10 Language Dictionary* (Adlard Coles Nautical) is a good buy.

Surprisingly, our biggest communication problems have been in Holland where, although English is widely spoken, no Dutch lock keeper (on a major commercial waterway) has ever responded to our radio calls in either English or pidgin Dutch!

The CEVNI, Rhine and Danube Commissions have various official languages, but only French is common to all three. A knowledge of some French is, therefore, useful everywhere and near indispensable if you intend to venture very far along the Danube.

Are there any rules about fishing in certain areas?

In most places you are permitted to fish, provided that you buy a permit. In France, look for village shops displaying a sign 'Permis de Peche en Vente Ici'. In Belgium you can buy permits at post offices. Elsewhere, ask at locks, town halls or Tourist Information Offices. In certain Scandinavian lakes (Sweden's enormous Lake Vatern, for example) you do not need a permit.

How much can I expect to pay for food and drink?

In general, starting with France as a datum, prices increase as you travel through Belgium, Holland, Germany, Sweden and Norway. Prices also increase as you pass through France from North to South. We have found that even Gouda cheese costs more in Holland than in France and Belgium! In some Dutch, German and Scandinavian supermarkets, prices are marked per half kilo. Don't get caught out!

All alcoholic beverages are cheapest in France, unless you desert the canals and voyage to Spain, where even pastis is cheaper than in its homeland. Northern France also produces some excellent strong beers (try Septante Cinq), but Belgium is the absolute Queen of Europe's beer producers. If you are a connoisseur, stocking up there is a must; they come in every strength and colour, from pale and potent to black and immensely potent!

Some towns – especially in Holland – have supermarkets on their quays if these are well frequented by barges; in other places grocery boats will come out to you. In neither case will you get the best bargains, since they deal with a captive market. The same applies to shops adjacent to touristic canals. Getting out the bike and going to where the locals shop is the best bet.

If you are on a budget, look out for Aldi and Lidl shops. When we wrote the first edition Aldi markets were only to be seen in Holland, Germany and the north of France. Today, they and Lidl shops have proliferated and stretched over more of the Continent.

What sort of clothing should I take with me?

Deciding what clothes to take is a tricky one. We once packed winter woollies for an early cruise to north Holland, only to find that temperatures had actually risen from a morning minus 2°C at Lille (northern France) to an afternoon plus 32°C in Hasselt (northern Holland). Since then we've opted for wearing layers!

Generally speaking, casual clothes (jeans, sweatshirts, t-shirts, and of course non-slip shoes) are all you need, but have one set of smart clothes – someone may invite you to their home for dinner!

Will I need heating on my boat?

Whether you need to fit a heater largely depends on you, your boat, where you go and where your galley is. We can count on one hand the number of times we've used our Epsbacher heater, which ducts warm air through the boat. On cold evenings, we cook a meal and the heat from the oven soon warms the main cabin. The aft cabin occupants have always preferred hot water bottles to a stifling atmosphere.

US visitors to the European waterways

We've met many Americans cruising continental waterways, many in hired cruisers, some in sailing boats they crossed the Atlantic with, a few who had their motor cruisers shipped to the continent and several in boats they bought when they arrived.

If you are going to hire a boat, it's really a question of studying the brochures and picking a waterway which offers the sort of things that interest you; brochures from the tourist office of the country or region concerned will help you choose.

The people we've met in sailing yachts have mostly been on their way to the Med, and in many cases were regretting that they ever thought it would be a good idea to explore inland France on the way. Their problems have mainly been caused by a deeper than desirable draft. We have also met some who acquired a compromise sailing boat, a relatively shallow draft vessel – often a bilge keeler – and had not enjoyed their Atlantic passage. The truth is that there is no such thing as a sailing boat which is right for both sea passages and canal work, so our advice would be don't try to find one. Make the decision as to whether you want to sail the Med, the Atlantic, the Baltic etc, or whether you want to roam inland, and choose your boat accordingly. If you decide to ship your own motor cruiser over you'll find details of companies which provide this service in the Appendix.

Many Americans have made excellent choices in the boats they have purchased on the continent, the majority having bought in Holland; a course we can definitely recommend because of the vast choice in all price ranges and sizes. Others have bought what might, at first thought, seem an excellent choice, an ex-hire cruiser, and found it was not such a good idea as it seemed.

Hire boats are purpose built to do a specific job, to enable a group of people, often with minimal boat handling skills, to have a very comfortable holiday on a canal with little or no commercial traffic. They are not designed to cope with waters churned by frequent passing barges, nor fast flowing waterways. If you want to leave a boat on a specific waterway and visit it for a summer holiday each year, a hire boat formerly used on the same waterway will provide you with a wonderful base. If you want to be free to get to other waterways, wherever they might be, you need a different sort of boat. We know of one person who had bought his ex-hire boat on the Canal du Midi and thoroughly enjoyed his visits to France, until he decided it was time to move on from that waterway. Thinking that the boat would be equally suitable for other canals, he had it transported by road to the mouth of the Loire and launched there. Not realising how difficult this river is, he ran aground twice whilst trying to progress up river and was then swept backwards because his boat's engine had never been intended to cope with such flows. We met him on the river Mayenne, onto which he had eventually been towed, and he and his family were decidedly chastened by the experience.

The next part of the chapter seeks to address many of the most frequently asked questions about bringing your own boat to Europe.

Will I have to pay import duty or VAT?

Boats which are intended to be re-exported eventually can temporarily be brought into the Customs Territory of the European Community (ECCT) and used for private purposes without customs duties or Value Added Tax (VAT) needing to be paid. The proviso is that this can only be done by persons who are non EU residents, to use the official term by those who are 'established outside that territory'.

The boats concerned have to undergo a 'temporary importation procedure' (TI) with Customs and the period of use in the Customs Territory is limited in time. When that time is up the boat has to leave; in official language this period is called 'the period of discharge'. Re-exportation is the usual way of 'discharging'. If the boat does not leave before the end of that time then customs duty and VAT become due.

A boat is temporarily imported into the ECCT and not into an individual Member State, so it can move between Member States without further customs formalities during the period allowed.

How is my yacht placed under 'temporary importation'?

Simply crossing the frontier into the Customs Territory of the Community automatically places it under TI, but some countries may require you to make an oral or written customs declaration. On rare occasions you might be asked to provide some kind of security or guarantee to cover payment of the customs duties and VAT that would become due if the boat does not leave the EU.

How long can my yacht stay in the ECCT without duty and VAT being paid?

In technical terms, the standard period for discharge for privately used means of sea and inland waterway transport is 18 months. There are, however, ways in which this can be extended. Here is the official European Commission article on this:

1 The Customs authorities shall determine the period within which import goods must have been re-exported or assigned a new Customs-approved

treatment or use. Such period must be long enough for the objective of authorized use to be achieved.

2 Without prejudice to special periods, the maximum period during which goods may remain under the temporary importation procedure shall be 24 months. The Customs authorities may, however, determine shorter periods with the agreement of the person concerned.

3 However, where exceptional circumstances so warrant, the Customs authorities may, at the request of the person concerned and within reasonable limits, extend the periods referred to in paragraphs 1 and 2 in order to permit the authorized use.

As you can see it is not exactly cut and dried and there is a very good reason for that. Customs authorities are not interested in preventing bona fide tourists from visiting their countries; they are interested in catching people who are cheating the tax system. You may have heard frightening stories of yachts being impounded and people fined; we have heard them too. We have investigated several such stories and, without exception to date, the yacht owners concerned were either cheating the system, or had told some fictitious story – which had been proved false - to a Customs Officer, or had simply gone on cruising for years without ever obtaining authorisation.

The best advice we can give you is to be above board. You are in Europe to see Europe, so say so, and tell the Customs people how long you feel you need to remain in Europe in order to explore every country you would like to visit. The UK authorities tend to be somewhat rigid when applying regulations which give scope for discretion, but many others will bend over backwards to accommodate you.

As a last resort, you can always leave the European Community Customs Territory and then return to start a new holiday. The Commission states that 'You are not limited to a single period of temporary import. You can sail the yacht out of the EU and when you come back again for another holiday a new period of temporary importation can begin. The Customs rules do not provide for a 'minimum period' during which the goods must remain outside of the Customs Territory of the EU.'

Curiously, you don't even have to leave Europe to leave the Customs Territory; Gibraltar and the Spanish cities of Ceuta and Mellila in North Africa are in the EU but not in the Customs Territory. However – although they do not apply VAT – Jersey and Guernsey *are* within the Customs Territory. With EU membership on the increase, we recommend that you get a list of countries within the Territory from the EU's Permanent Delegation to the United States (see Appendix).

What US competence certificate will be valid in Europe?

The simple answer at the time of writing is none and we have come across people who have gone to extraordinary lengths to get around this. Some, having been told that a commercial certificate from the US Coast Guard will be accepted on French inland waters, have gone to great trouble to get one only to find on arrival that they were misinformed. Others have acquired a UK accommodation address and used it to obtain a UK International Certificate of Competence (ICC), which is only supposed to be issued to British residents or those genuinely working in Britain. This is not a good idea because – as said above – temporary importation of yachts can only be done by persons who are established outside Europe's Customs Territory. You cannot claim to be established outside Europe for the purpose of temporary importation and inside it for the purpose of obtaining an ICC; to do so is likely to result in problems with one authority or other. Sensible US visitors to date have acquired a Dutch or French certificate, which are recognised in the other country on a basis of reciprocity.

By the time you read this, we hope that the problem of an ICC for American citizens will have been resolved. The ICC scheme was worked out by the United Nations Principal Working Party on Inland Transport and the US is a member. We have been working with a US Sailing School (see Appendix) to have an official way for a US ICC to be issued.

Schengen Travelling in Europe has been simplified with the introduction of the Schengen visa, since visitors to the Schengen area enjoy the many advantages of this unified visa system.

With a Schengen visa, visitors can enter one country and travel freely throughout the Schengen zone. Internal border controls have disappeared; there are few or no stops and checks. This means that internal air, road, train and waterway travels are handled as domestic trips.

To visit only one Schengen country, you must apply at the Embassy or Consulate of that particular country. You apply at the Embassy or Consulate responsible for the state where you live.

If you intend to visit several Schengen countries (for full list see page 41), you must apply for a visa at the Embassy or Consulate of the country which is your main destination.

If you intend to visit several Schengen countries but do not have a main destination, you should apply for a visa at the Embassy or Consulate of the country which is your first point of entry.

What's different in Europe?

Electrical supply
The US mains supply is 110 volts; in Europe it is between 220 and 240 volts, so you cannot just plug into a shore power supply, leaving aside the fact that the plugs are different. Contact your local electrical supplier for details.

Credit cards

Firstly check that you have an international version. You'll also probably be surprised to learn that continental Europe is somewhat ahead of the US in credit card technology, having long since embraced the 'puce', that sort of 'blob' that means the card can be read by simply being pushed into a special machine and not just on the 'swipe' bar. At the time of writing, this was not universal in the US, nor in the UK, so check with your bank to see if they can supply one; it will save you hassle in various places.

Mobile phones

If you are staying in a particular country for a while, it makes sense to get a local number for local calls like booking a restaurant table or checking whether spares are available. Many continental supermarkets can arrange for you to sign up with a local service provider, if they can't there will be a local specialist shop that can and all that needs to be done is to change the card in your own phone. One word of warning, ask to see a map of the areas covered by a particular provider before signing up, or you could find yourself without service on parts of your planned route.

Such minor problems and irritants apart, the charm of cruising Europe is that it *is* different which is part of its charm.

We recommend you also read Chapter 4 on 'things to know before you go', because in many ways the continent is 'foreign' to UK citizens too!

Internet services

This is an area where things are moving very fast and if, like many of us, you have come to rely on it, cruising anywhere can be a problem unless money is no object.

E-mail only services

The SailMail Association is a non-profit association of yacht owners that operates and maintains a network of private coast stations in the Maritime Mobile Radio Service. The Association provides radioprinter (eg Internet e-mail) communications for its members on a cooperative basis, in order to meet the private business and operational needs of the members' yachts.

For sailors who don't need the features of the commercial systems, SailMail offers a simple and affordable solution.

Passing messages between a radio connection and the internet requires some special software at both ends of the radio link. The AirMail program at the user's end is a complete Windows 95/98/NT/2000/ME/XP messaging program, useful for SailMail and for the Ham networks, which handles message creation/editing and mostly automates the radio link. A number of SailMail members successfully run AirMail on Apple computers using Virtual PC or similar PC emulation programs.

The station's computer provides the companion functionality and responds to a connect request from the user. Any messages that have been received from Internet e-mail are downloaded to the vessel, and messages heading towards the Internet are formatted and sent. There are limitations on the messages that can be handled, due to the low bandwidth of the radio network. Messages are limited to plain-text email messages of a length of 5kB (two text pages) or less, and members are requested to use less than 10 minutes per day of SailMail station time. Members who use Pactor-III can receive e-mail messages of up to 10kB in length.

The only difficult part of setting up a Pactor station is the variety of equipment that is available, none of which uses compatible connections. This means that cables need to be made up especially for each installation, which is the main source of problems.

Three components are needed to set up a SailMail station: a radio transceiver (and antenna), a Pactor HF-modem, and a computer with the appropriate software. The HF-modem is the only specialized piece of equipment, and is essentially a radio modem, similar in concept to the ubiquitous computer modem used for telephone connections. The HF-modem generates the audio signals that are sent via the radio transmitter, and decodes the incoming audio signals from the radio receiver. The primary connections between the HF modem and the radio are two audio signals (audio in and audio out), plus a PTT (push-to-talk) signal to tell the radio when to transmit. Transmitting and receiving digital signals is similar to voice, and most modern marine SSB radios will do the job.

More comprehensive communication services

Inmarsat Inmarsat launched the new F55 Fleet service along with the more powerful F77 product in early 2002. It offers leisure and small commercial vessels outstanding voice connections worldwide and high-speed data and Internet connections over 90 percent of marine cruising routes, shipping lanes, and all of the most popular maritime regions around the globe.

Two distinct data services are available with the F55 Fleet; mobile ISDN, or Mobile Packet Data Service (MPDS). These services are provided using Inmarsat's powerful spot beam technology. Designed for short-burst data transmissions, MPDS is perfect for receiving e-mail, logging onto and working within a company intranet, or browsing the web. And with its 'pay per bit' pricing, users are charged only for the amount of the data sent and received, not by connection time. As a result, a vessel can remain connected via e-mail or the Internet 24 hours a day, 7 days a week at no additional cost, making maritime Internet access a far more relaxing experience. The high-capacity mobile ISDN channel provides a constant data stream at speeds as fast as 64 Kbps, making it ideal for phone and fax service, video conferencing, and transmitting large files and images. ISDN usage is charged on a per-minute basis.

The Inmarsat Fleet F33 service was launched in early 2003 and aims to fill the gap between the existing Inmarsat Mini-M service and the global Inmarsat Fleet F77 service. It will provide the light marine market with improved data communications from equipment suitable for the demands of today's commercial and leisure fleet. Satellite communications are increasingly being used by marine vessels in order to access online connectivity with the onshore world.

Iridium Iridium's satellite network offers fully global coverage including oceans and Polar Regions and enables beside pager services via short message receiver-reliable speech and data communication with bandwidth up to 2,4 to 10 Kbps by using relatively small and favourable mobile satellite phones.

Iridium offers prepaid and scratch & phone services. Specially designed Iridium prepaid services for low and high users are showing an increasing popularity in the maritime ambience. They offer cost control without causing administration and especially favourable minutes/hardware comb packages.

Prepaid offers are ideal for users who are not regularly using the Iridium voice and data communication services, only sporadically, eg yacht owner, adventure traveller, hobby sailors and business people with seasonal business. Iridium scratch & phone cards are offering optimum conditions for users, who are sharing an existing Iridium unit, by using the handset and a scratch & phone card via a SIM card and a personnel PIN, without buying a new installation. The scratch & phone solution can be used in the whole Iridium network world-wide, furthermore it is possible to make and to charge phone calls of the ship's crew in a post paid modus, because post-paid and scratch & phone calls are separated automatically.

Other services include the data compression and transport software SkyFile, which will be available soon for Iridium data transmission too, as well as the new 'Short Burst Data Service' (Mobile Packet Data Service), which enables data transfer in packets of up to 1,960 bytes (Mobile Packet Data Service) via Iridium's handsets.

Single-sideband radio (SSB) Icom UK Ltd offers the IC-M802 marine single-sideband (SSB) transceiver for customers who operate or sail under a non EU flag. This product at the moment does not have type approval for the UK for UK vessels. It's a marine SSB which includes Digital Selective Calling (DSC) for automated ship-to-ship and ship-to-shore messaging that doubles as a powerful MF/HF radio transceiver, and triples as an e-mail conduit for wireless computer-to-computer connections and a European version was expected to be available shortly at the time of writing.

Many mariners want e-mail capabilities over marine SSB. The new IC-M802 builds in automatic filter selection without the need for additional hardware. It is ready to e-mail as soon as you select your multimode data controller (a radio modem).

Reasonably priced, full Internet access wherever you are must be one of the most important future developments which will influence people in deciding whether they can take that extended inland cruise or not. When it is available, at prices similar to current land access, extended cruising will no longer be the province of only the rich or retired. Further information is available on www.boatsyachtsmarinas.com, where all developments in this field are published.

European waterway rules (CEVNI)

The basis of most European inland waterway rules is the United Nations CEVNI (*Code European des Voies Navigables Interieures*). Certain countries and even individual waterways may have their own supplementary (sometimes even contradictory) rules, such as RPNR (*Reglement de Police pour la Navigation du Rhin*), but CEVNI remains the fundamental base on which safe, competent waterway practice is founded.

Strictly speaking, much of CEVNI applies only to vessels over 65 feet (20 metres) long, but it is something that every inland waterway user should know and understand. On the Continent, it is essential that *plaisanciers* are aware of the intentions of commercial vessels. On the UK's narrow canals, the manoeuvres of a narrow boat are similar to those of a commercial barge (*péniche*) on a smaller French waterway. In each case, vessels have to enter locks with just centimetres to spare and they have to manoeuvre, relative to similar vessels, in very confined waters. The fact that the *péniche* has over five times the carrying capacity of the narrow boat is irrelevant, because everything else is to a similar scale. On main waterways, knowing and understanding CEVNI brings that essential understanding of commercial vessels' actions. On the narrow UK network, using CEVNI as role model, rather than regulation, is an excellent approach.

Anyone who took a car on the road without knowing which side to drive on, who had priority, and what particular signs and lights meant, would be universally condemned as a dangerous lunatic. Yet, strangely enough, some of those doing the condemning would think nothing of cruising down a waterway 'road' without having a clue about the signs, rules etc. Don't be one of them. It is easier to stop, steer and reverse a car than a boat, so you could say that knowing what you are doing on the inland waterways is even more important than knowing what you are doing on the road.

The RYA Book of EuroRegs for Inland Waterways (Adlard Coles Nautical) is a handy reference to CEVNI/RPNR, and in this and subsequent chapters the important rules will be quoted, explained and described in practical terms. First, though, we need an explanation of some canal lore and terminology.

A bit of history

The size of continental vessels matches the size of waterways on the Continent and the history of the French canalised River Aa (the first major canal that most beginners encounter) illustrates that link, as well as the importance of waterways, to continental economies. The Aa was first canalised in medieval times, but the present canalised river, known as the Canal de Neufosse, was constructed in the late eighteenth century as part of a northern network that linked Channel ports with Lille and Paris. To link l'Aa to the River Lys, a staircase of locks was built at Fontinettes to overcome the 13 metre level difference. Traffic levels rapidly rose, and by 1855, when it had exceeded 380 000 tons per annum, the staircase had become a serious bottleneck. During the next 20 years, traffic more than doubled and, to compound the inadequacies of Fontinettes, a law was passed in 1879 stating that all French locks would be at least 38.5 metres long. Fontinettes' locks were 4 metres too short, so local authorities overcame the problems by building a boat lift, to the approved dimensions, which could carry one barge up whilst another came down.

The 1879 law stemmed from a plan to rationalise the entire French network. As locks were upgraded to the new dimensions, commercial users, anxious to carry as much cargo as possible, had vessels built that could enter the locks and lifts with just centimetres to spare, and these wooden barges became known as the standard Freycinet *péniche*, after the author of the national plan.

Freycinet's heritage lives on in a network of smaller canals and rivers which still criss-cross much of central and northern France but, on the Neufosse, traffic continued to augment. But by the 1950s, Fontinettes was again a serious bottleneck, so in 1962 work began on a new lock. When it went into service in 1969, Fontinettes' capacity had increased tenfold and the Canal de Neufosse could be used by vessels of 110 metres long, with a beam of 11.4 metres.

Continental waterway classifications

In 1992, a UN Resolution defined classification criteria for commercially important European waterways. Those criteria were the length and beam of the largest vessel which could use a waterway – the beam being the most important consideration. The modern equivalent of the sailing, or horsedrawn, Freycinet *péniche* has a powerful engine and a steel hull, but in size and appearance it has scarcely changed in over 100 years. Waterways which cannot accept vessels larger than a *péniche* are Class 1 and they still exist in Belgium as well as France. With rare exceptions, Holland's smallest commercial waterways are Class 2, ie they can accept a *kampenaar* which looks like a *péniche* but is 50 metres long with a beam of 6.6 metres and capacity of up to 650 tons. Small German waterways tend to be bigger still – Class 3 – and can be used by *Gustav Koenigs* – vessels of 67 to 80 metres long, with a beam of 8.2 metres and a capacity of up to 1000 tons.

Péniche, *kampenaaren* and *Gustav Koenigs* are the local 'delivery vans' and 'light lorries' of the waterways; they take corn to mills, deliver bulk coal to quay-side merchants and ferry factory products to distribution points. These boat types and corresponding waterway classifications refer to the canals and rivers which are west of the Elbe; dimensions of Class 1 to Class 3 waterways to the east of the Elbe are slightly different. Waterways of Classes 4 to 7 are usually of international importance and the UN Resolution quotes standard classification criteria throughout Europe. As a minimum these waterways can be used by *Johann Welker* vessels of 80 metres by 9.5 metres, and on Class 5 and up, you will see *Large Rhine Ships* – 110 metres by 11.4 metres – and possibly sea-going *RoRos* of up to 140 metres by 15 metres. However, by far the biggest vessels you are likely to meet will be pushed convoys, made up from a powerful 'pusher' (sometimes more than one) containing an engine room and crew accommodation, pushing one or several lighters. In our experience, the most regularly encountered are single pusher/lighter combinations 110 metres x 11.4 metres with a 3000 ton capacity. Not that long ago, great convoys of lighters, pulled by a tug, were regular sights on the Rhine but now tugged convoys are rare on Western waterways. However, on Class 7 parts of the Danube, such convoys are the rule, not the exception, and their dimensions can be staggering. Some are 650 metres long by 45 metres wide, with 32 000 ton capacity, others are shorter but wider!

Take it seriously

Having absorbed figures which, by narrowboat standards, are truly enormous, you will have realised that except for a few short river stretches, coming in from the sea, and even fewer stretches of canal – such as the Aire and Calder – the UK has few waterways which attain even the minimum dimensions for a UN classification. You may, therefore, be wondering why I have bothered to describe continental waterway standards when it is obvious that only those with exceptionally large or deep-draft vessels would ever have to ask 'Can I go along that waterway?'

The answer is that I want to dispel a notion, which prevails in certain UK circles, that inland waterway cruising is a low skill pursuit requiring little preparation, boatmanship or knowledge. Of course, people with little skill and knowledge do cruise inland waters, but just as many put to sea without understanding the International Collision Regulations, navigation techniques, buoy recognition, boat mechanics etc. That is one of the reasons for a staggering cost to the RNLI for launches to pleasure craft which have got lost, become stranded, broken down and so on. The difference between sea and inland cruising is that, unlike sea goers, inland cruisers are often in very close proximity to giant vessels and, if something unexpected happens, inland cruisers do not have the luxury of sea room, so have little time in which to react correctly. For peace of mind, familiarise yourself with the rules, have good maps and make sure your boat is well maintained.

Draft

On good overall maps, continental waterways will be colour coded, according to classification. The UN Resolution on classification states the maximum recommended draft for a vessel which is likely to use a particular Class of waterway and this will also be stated on a good map. In most cases, this will be far more than your vessel is likely to draw, but those with sailing boats and other vessels with more than the ideal draft should be a little cautious. Figures quoted for recommended draft are based on water levels which are achieved on 240 days per year and there is nothing to say that you won't be there on one of the other 125 days, so if in doubt, take local advice. Secondly, waterways may have local areas of reduced draft. These are marked on the UN map, published following the classification, which covers waterways from the UK to Russia and is published under ISBN No 92-1-016-299-4.

Just to confuse?

It might have been better if the UN Resolution had, like British Waterways, referred to Standard 1, 2, 3 etc waterways because – when that Resolution was formulated – the expressions Class 1 and Class 2 waterways were already in use in CEVNI, where they mean something quite different: rivers are generally Class 1 and canals, lakes, meers etc are usually Class 2. So the Rhine is a Class 6 waterway under Resolution 30 (the one about classifications by vessel size) and a Class 1 waterway under Resolution 24 (the adoption of CEVNI). In CEVNI, there are different 'rules of the road' on Class 1 and 2 waterways, so remember that when we talk about rules for meeting, signals used in reduced visibility etc, we are talking about the CEVNI classification.

Strange terminology

It isn't just abroad that canal terminology may be 'foreign'; the UK also has some strange terms. For example, it is impossible to turn a long boat in a narrow canal, so areas had to be made where the boats could be manoeuvred round. These were called 'winding holes', a name derived from sailing barge terminology, where crews still talk of 'winding' rather than 'tacking'. 'Paddles' is another colloquial British term for the mechanism which lets water into and out of locks. Even the word 'lock' is unique to the UK, for almost everywhere else, a sluice is a schluss, a slus, a sluss or at least something vaguely similar, like a French *écluse*. Incidentally, the wind in 'winding' is the sort which blows, not the way you turn something.

CEVNI signs and signals

In 1982, the United Nations' Economic Commission for Europe accepted that a standard sign and signal system, known as SIGNI (*Signaux des Voies Interieures*), would be adopted throughout Europe to ensure that language would not be a barrier to international waterway travel. The signs have been incorporated into CEVNI and are now used throughout most of the mainland, though parts of Russia, Moldova and Poland lag behind when it comes to standardising signs. However, those countries whose commercial inland waterways are only extensions of seaways have scarcely adopted the system at all.

Britain, for example, has in the main developed its own system. Fortunately, in many cases, the signs are similar, but there are some important differences – and not knowing about those differences could get you into trouble if you are used to one code and not the other.

Take weirs, for example. British Waterways signpost weirs extremely clearly, with large motorway-style panels (see Fig 6.1). If you went to the Continent, expecting to get an equally clear warning, you could be taken by surprise. The simple blue and white panel in Fig 6.2 is the CEVNI weir sign!

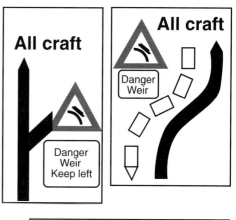
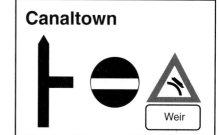

Fig 6.1 UK weir signs.

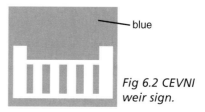

Fig 6.2 CEVNI weir sign.

No entry signs

Conversely, a regular continental canal user could end up in a problem area by assuming that 'No Entry' signs mean precisely the same in the UK as they do under CEVNI.

In the UK the red and white round sign means 'No Entry' (see Fig 6.3). It applies to all boats and is often used to mark danger zones. On the Continent it also means 'No Entry', but it is mainly used to mark areas that are not easily navigable, so it does not apply to small (non-motorised) boats such as dinghies.

The CEVNI sign for a dangerous and/or prohibited area is a horizontal white bar on an oblong red background. It means 'No Entry', 'No Passing Through' etc, and is referred to as a 'General Prohibitory Sign'. It is sometimes used in the UK.

The CEVNI sign in Fig 6.3 – a black bar on a white panel, with red surround – also means 'No Passing', but only applies in certain circumstances. Those circumstances are usually obvious. For example, when the sign is displayed at a lock, it means 'Stop, if the lights are red'. When the circumstances in which you have to stop are unclear, they are given on a panel below the sign. For example, the German word ZOLL means 'Stop, if required to do so by the Customs'.

Mandatory signs

With a few exceptions, whatever country you are in, signs that tell you that you *must not* do something are white, with a red border and red diagonal, and those that say you *must* do something are white with a red border, but no diagonal. On the Continent almost all signs are rectangular; in the UK they are often round or triangular.

Most of the symbols used on signs, like the one which means 'No mooring', are self-explanatory, but, some, like the UK one which means 'You must not pump out your toilet holding tanks', are less obvious! (See Fig 6.4.)

Other red-bordered signs tell you about restriction in draft, air draft and canal dimensions. They all have black triangles in the sign, so are easily remembered as a group (see Fig 6.5). Often, there will be numbers to indicate headroom, or some other dimension. In the UK the unit of measurement is usually given. On the Continent, it is *always* in metres, so the unit is not stated.

Advisory signs

The other main group of signs have white symbols on a light-blue background. These are signs that inform you about something, and thus help you to make a decision. For example, if you saw a sign showing a white water skier on a blue background, it would be wise not to moor if you wanted a peaceful evening (see Fig 6.6). Light-blue signs often have a red-bordered counterpart.

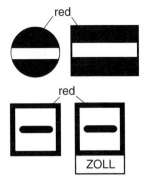

Fig 6.3 Left: No entry signs. Right: No passing signs.

No mooring   No pumping out

Fig 6.4 Mandatory signs.

| Canal narrows | Reduced depth |
| Channel is 10m from bank | Reduced height |

Fig 6.5 Red-bordered restriction signs.

No windsurfing   Windsurfing permitted

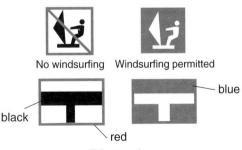

Tributary signs

Fig 6.6 Above: These red/white and blue/white signs are opposites. Below: Although different colours these two signs mean the same thing.

Most red-bordered signs say the opposite of their blue counterpart, but paradoxically some say almost the same thing. For example, both tributary signs in Fig 6.6 say 'You are approaching a more major canal'. The red-bordered one also tells masters of large vessels that, before joining the major canal, they must make sure that boats already on that canal will not have to alter their speed or course because of their actions. In truth, regardless of whether the sign was red-bordered or light-blue, a cautious entry into a major waterway is essential. It is rather like hurtling out of a country lane into the path of a lorry, then saying, 'Well, there wasn't a give-way sign'.

Although light-blue signs are used on some UK waterways, the majority of British Waterways information signs have black symbols on white backgrounds. Many of these are self-explanatory but a few are rather obscure! For example, the signs in Fig 6.7 are very similar, but they have different meanings.

Rubbish disposal Sewage disposal

Fig 6.7 Two similar signs with quite different meanings!

Supplementary information

Signs often have additional information on a panel attached to the main sign (see Fig 6.8). Triangular panels on the side of the main sign are often placed at the start of the restriction (or permission) and tell you how long it goes on for. The first example in Fig 6.8 means 'No anchoring for 400 metres'.

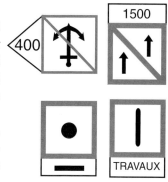

Rectangular panels, at the top of the main sign, indicate how far ahead a restriction (or permission) will commence. The second example means 'No overtaking zone, 1500 metres ahead'.

Rectangular panels at the bottom of the main sign give more information about what that sign says. In the third example, the main sign says

Fig 6.8 Panels attached to main signs give more information.

'Make a sound signal' and the panel says that the signal should be one long blast. In the fourth example, the main sign means 'Look out!' or 'Pay attention'. The French word on the panel tells you what you should be looking out for, ie work being carried out.

Another group of signs is often used on fixed bridges and sometimes lights are used instead of signs. For example, in Paris, where *bateaux mouches* travel the Seine by night, yellow lights are used to recommend which bridge arch should be used (see Fig 6.9).

Berthing restrictions

On smaller canals and rivers it isn't hard to find a pleasant (and free) place to spend the night. However, on international waterways it is a different story, partly

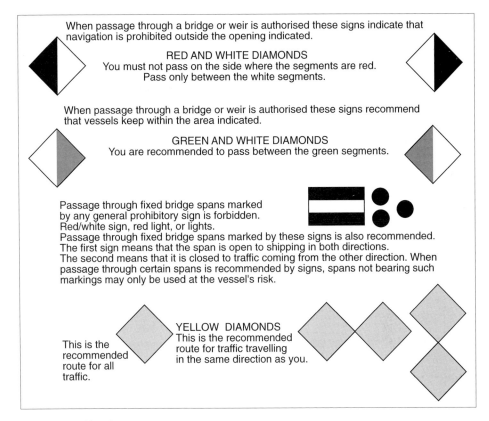

When passage through a bridge or weir is authorised these signs indicate that navigation is prohibited outside the opening indicated.

RED AND WHITE DIAMONDS
You must not pass on the side where the segments are red.
Pass only between the white segments.

When passage through a bridge or weir is authorised these signs recommend that vessels keep within the area indicated.

GREEN AND WHITE DIAMONDS
You are recommended to pass between the green segments.

Passage through fixed bridge spans marked by any general prohibitory sign is forbidden. Red/white sign, red light, or lights.
Passage through fixed bridge spans marked by these signs is also recommended. The first sign means that the span is open to shipping in both directions. The second means that it is closed to traffic coming from the other direction. When passage through certain spans is recommended by signs, spans not bearing such markings may only be used at the vessel's risk.

This is the recommended route for all traffic.

YELLOW DIAMONDS
This is the recommended route for traffic travelling in the same direction as you.

Fig 6.9 Fixed bridges.

because 24-hour traffic isn't conducive to sleep, and partly because you are likely to see a host of signs saying 'Don't berth/moor/anchor here'. 'Berthing' is defined as 'making fast (directly or indirectly) to the bank, or anchoring'.

You must always berth as close to the bank as your draft and local conditions permit and in a manner that does not obstruct shipping. Your boat must be secured in a way that ensures that it will not change position and thus constitute a possible danger, or obstruction, to shipping. Always take into account the possible effects of wind, tide (if any), water level, suction and wash.

Do not berth under bridges and high voltage electric cables. On the Continent, the presence of high voltage electric cables is often indicated by a white discharge symbol on a blue background. In the UK a black discharge symbol is shown on a yellow triangle with black surround.

Do not berth in, or near, narrow channels, nor in one that would become narrow if you berthed there! Do not berth at entries to, or exits from, tributaries, on the course of ferry boats, on the route to a landing stage, nor in a designated turning area.

With one exception, the red bordered CEVNI signs which prohibit berthing have a diagonal bar through one of these symbols: P = No making fast or anchoring.

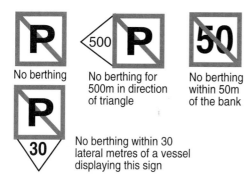

No berthing

No berthing for 500m in direction of triangle

No berthing within 50m of the bank

No berthing within 30 lateral metres of a vessel displaying this sign

Fig 6.10 Berthing restrictions.

Bollard = No making fast (but you may anchor). Anchor = No anchoring (but you may make fast). Conversely, when one of those symbols is shown in white, on a blue background, you may berth in areas where berthing would normally be prohibited, at the side where the sign is placed.

Another group of berthing signs have various triangles and/or diamonds on a blue background. As far as you are concerned they mean 'Don't moor here, this is reserved for commercial vessels'. Heed this because (a) commercial vessels need these spaces (b) some are reserved for vessels with dangerous cargoes and you have an obligation to keep away from them. You will find drawings of these signs in Appendix A.

Trailing anchors

The sign prohibiting anchoring is sometimes displayed in places where you are unlikely to want to anchor. In these instances, the signs really mean 'Do not trail anchors, under any circumstances'. In many cases, they tell you why, on an additional panel. For example, the Belgian word BUIZEN indicates that there are pipelines under water. Even when the 'No anchoring' sign is not displayed, trailing anchors, cables and chains, other than when making small stopping or manoeuvring movements, is forbidden.

Trailing anchors, cables or chains at or near a weir is strictly prohibited. There are circumstances (we have never encountered them) when passage through an opening in a weir is permitted. In those circumstances, the permitted passage is indicated by displaying the green and white general permission sign or green lights to either side of the opening.

Prescribed courses

In certain waterway sections you are instructed by mandatory signs to follow a certain course (see Figs 6.11a and 6.11b).

Traffic lights

Lights are also used to control traffic in one-way systems and at bridges, locks etc (see Fig 6.12).

Two red lights, one above the other, mean 'out of service'. This could mean several things – from 'You've arrived during the almost sacred continental lunch

Go in the
direction of
the arrow

Move to the left
of the channel

Move to the right
of the channel

Keep to the left
of the channel

Keep to the right
of the channel

Cross the
channel to port

Cross the channel
to starboard

Fig 6.11a Where the course is prescribed and espe-cially in sections marked by the last two signs, upstream vessels must not impede the progress of downstream vessels. If necessary, upstream vessels must slow down or even stop to let downstream vessels manoeuvre.

period' to 'Sorry, the gates are jammed'. Your maps and guides should tell you if you have arrived at a lock or bridge outside operating hours. At other times, when you see superimposed red lights, your best course of action is to moor and go ashore to find out the reason for the closure.

Fig 6.11b The end of a section, with a pre-scribed course, may be indicated by this blue and white 'end of restriction' sign.

In the UK, an amber light is sometimes displayed at manned locks and bridges when the operator is absent. You may be allowed to operate the obstacle yourself (consult your waterway guide, or notices posted at the lock or bridge), but when-ever you see an amber light you should proceed with caution. There may be some unexpected reason for the operator's absence such as a problem just beyond a bridge.

Two red lights side by side, or a single red light (Fig 6.12), indicate that the lock/bridge/one-way section is not open for you at this moment. That does not mean that it won't be open in a few minutes' time, so you have to decide whether to moor or not. We always try to avoid mooring, especially in urban areas where the usual canalside underwater hazards tend to be augmen-ted by supermarket trolleys, bikes etc.

One red light over another means lock, bridge etc out of service.

These red lights mean lock, bridge etc temporarily closed for you.

Red and green lights or one red lit, one extinguished means prepare to go.

Green lights mean proceed.

With a single-light system you don't get any warning about preparing to move; it's red for 'No go' one second, and green for 'Go' the next. When

Fig 6.12 Traffic lights.

the more common twin-light system is used, you should prepare to go when one red light is extinguished or when red and green lights are displayed side by side. Remember, these lights only mean 'Prepare to go', so don't make the mistake of casting off from a mooring as soon as you see them. At locks, for example, 'Prepare to go' lights are often displayed as soon as the lock starts to cycle towards you, so you could still have quite a wait. It is far better to stay tied up until you see clues about the state of the lock, such as a barge roof appearing or gates starting to open. *You must not enter a lock or tunnel, or pass through a bridge, whilst any red lights are showing. The signal to go is one or two green lights.*

Sound signals

Sound signals (other than bells) are normally given by mechanically operated devices, mounted in high unobstructed positions, but in most countries small craft may use a horn, or trumpet instead (unless they intend to navigate using radar). Small craft should only make the general sound signals (see Fig 6.13).

Commercial vessels use a number of other signals, and it is important to know what those signals mean as they tell you where a large vessel is likely to steer. Also, you might need to use one in an emergency. These additional signals will be covered when writing about the situations they are used in.

On commercial waterways, the use of sound signals other than those mentioned in CEVNI and local regulations, or the use of those signals in circumstances other than those they are meant for, is prohibited. The only exception is that vessels may communicate with each other, or with a shore station, using other signals. In doing so, they must not use signals that might be confused with

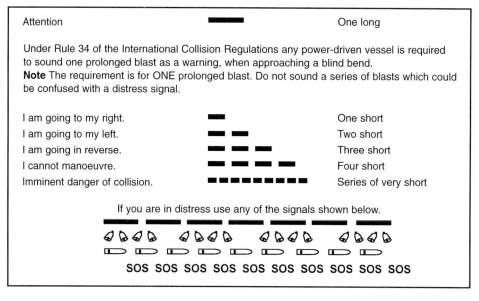

Fig 6.13 Sound signals.

regulation ones. That said, the UK does use other sound signals and these even vary according to which authority's waterways you are cruising on. The most common ones are given in Fig 6.14.

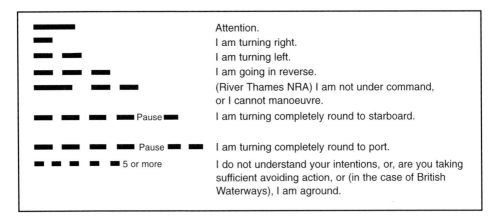

Attention.
I am turning right.
I am turning left.
I am going in reverse.
(River Thames NRA) I am not under command, or I cannot manoeuvre.
I am turning completely round to starboard.

I am turning completely round to port.
I do not understand your intentions, or, are you taking sufficient avoiding action, or (in the case of British Waterways), I am aground.

Fig 6.14 UK sound signals.

Signs and symbols displayed by other vessels

Some other important signs that you must be able to recognise are those displayed on boats, either by symbols or lights. There are several pages of these given in Appendix A, but Figs 6.15 to 6.16 give some that you should memorise.

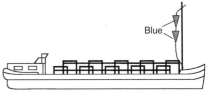

Fig 6.15 Displaying symbols.

Dangerous cargoes

Vessels carrying dangerous cargo display one, two or three blue cones (see Fig 6.15). You must not moor within 10 metres of a vessel with one blue cone (carrying inflammable materials), within 50 metres of a vessel with two blue cones (carrying ammoniac) or 100 metres of a vessel with three blue cones (carrying explosive materials). (In certain countries, one red cone is used instead of three blue ones, and two red cones in place of two blue ones.)

Certain berthing areas are reserved for vessels with dangerous cargoes. They are always marked with a blue and white sign; at least one blue cone is shown (full list in Appendix A). You must not moor at these berths.

Never try to enter a lock with a vessel with two or three blue cones; they are *never* locked with other vessels. When in a lock with a vessel with one blue cone, keep 10 metres away.

Passing other vessels

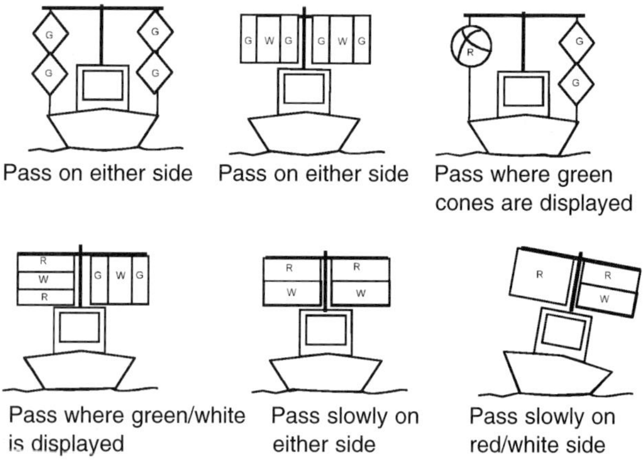

A vessel working in the channel that does not need protection from wash, and that may be passed on either side, displays green bicones or green and white flags.

If the green bicones or green/white flag are on one side, and a red ball or red and white flag is displayed on the other

Pass on either side   Pass on either side   Pass where green cones are displayed

Pass where green/white   Pass slowly on   Pass slowly on
is displayed   either side   red/white side

Fig 6.16 Passing vessels.

side, you must only pass down the side with the green signs. If a vessel is displaying any red over white sign, eg a red flag flying above a white one, you must slow down because it needs protection from wash.

When it is unsafe to pass down one side of a vessel, and the vessel needs protection from wash, it will display a red over white flag on the safe side and a red flag on the unsafe side.

The vessel passing signs/symbols described so far are illustrated in Fig 6.16. These signs are used throughout continental Europe and you may also see them on some UK river navigations. However, on British Waterways, vessels usually display a red flag on the side you must not pass and a white flag on the passing side.

Safety first

When compared with other modes of transport, canals come out exceedingly well from a safety point of view. However, where there is any water there is always potential danger, especially to children, so here are some safety do's and don't's:

- Make sure that all children and any non-swimming adults wear correctly fastened lifejackets when they are in any situation where they could fall into the water.
- Do impress upon children that they should not run about – especially when decks or lock surrounds are wet, increasing the chances of them slipping.
- Don't let anyone sit on a narrow boat's roof, or a conventional cruiser's coachroof, when passing through a lifting bridge or under a fixed bridge. A carelessly operated lifting bridge could descend on the boat and, at

fixed bridges, local children have been known to hurl missiles. When you are passing through any bridge, or into/out of a lock, remind anyone on deck that they should hold on. If you bump a wall or buttress, anyone not holding on could be bounced into the water.

- If someone does fall overboard, you must act quickly but calmly; there are no hard and fast rules about what you should do, because of the near-endless variation in circumstances. They may have fallen off the front or the back, the current may be with the boat or against you; they may be a good swimmer or a non-swimmer, they may be wearing a lifejacket or not. You have to decide what is the biggest threat (eg drowning, being swept over a weir, getting maimed by the propeller) and act accordingly. It is infinitely better not to fall in, so always hold on to grab rails when walking round the boat.

- If someone falls overboard in any DIY lock, close all paddles and throw them the nearest thing that floats. Obviously a lifebelt is best, but if you can't quickly reach it, an oar or a plastic-covered foam cushion would help give immediate extra buoyancy. If you are sharing a lock and other boats are running engines, yell 'Man overboard. Engines off' at the top of your voice and sound a series of long horn blasts (or other emergency signal). Then consider how to get the person out, depending on positions of ladders, state of lock etc. If someone falls overboard in a manned lock, throw something to help them float and yell (or radio) for assistance, whilst making a distress signal.

- Sensible lock and bridge procedures will help to ensure that you do not fall in. For example, never push or fend the boat off by leaning out and using your hands. Keep a boat hook handy and use it. Also, don't use your feet to fend off; if they slip, you could end up with a crushed leg.

- Never accept offers from passers-by to operate bridges or locks. They may know more than you, or they may know nothing. Never head for partly opened lock gates or movable bridges. If you go too early and the bridge or gate jams (half open), you might hit it.

- Never allow children to steer the boat and don't let them operate locks and bridges, or sit (alone) on lift bridges to keep them open. They can, of course, 'help' you with operations, but remember the lifejackets. If your work load is too high to supervise younger children properly, put them inside the cabin when negotiating any potentially hazardous situation.

- Wherever you are cruising, stopping at a bankside pub is one of the attractions, but it is best to stick to non-alcoholic drinks, until you've finished your day's cruising. British Waterways say that excess alcohol consumption is often mentioned in accident reports.

Cruising small canals and rivers

Rules about large vessels meeting on most rivers differ from those on other waterways, because river navigation creates special problems for both upstream and downstream vessels A vessel going with the current, especially a fast flow, is less controllable than one going against it. A vessel going against the current may need to keep to a particular bank, in order to overcome the flow. So, when meeting on rivers, downstream boats have priority (in the sense that upstream boats must leave them sufficient manoeuvring room), but upstream boats can choose which side they leave room on.

In practice, those rules cannot be applied to large vessels navigating small rivers, because there is not enough room, so we'll look at river rules later.

Meeting other boats

Always stay on the right, unless a sign, signal or authority tells you to do otherwise. If necessary, when meeting another boat, move further right and pass port to port. In the UK, you often see pleasure boats criss-crossing going upstream to take advantage of weaker currents inside bends. This is not good practice. You may be keeping a sharp lookout, but you can't guarantee that others are.

Approaching a bend on the 'wrong' side of a waterway used by pleasure boats is unwise, and on commercial waterways it could be dangerous. Unladen barges, hurrying to collect another cargo, assume a nose-up/back-down attitude. The bargee's view is obstructed by the cargo hold and he can only see what is ahead by leaning out of one side of the wheelhouse, then the other. When he expects to encounter another vessel he will station a lookout on the bow, but he may not know that a *plaisancier* is about to meander into his path (see Fig 7.1). For instance, you may have passed through a lock the previous afternoon, decided to moor for the rest of the day, and continued your journey the next morning. So if asked 'Are any boats coming the other way?' the lock keeper, having let you through some 12 hours previously, would say 'No' – and you might come round a corner to find a looming black shape, dead ahead.

Depending on circumstances, you would have to decide whether to steer sharp right to get into view, or veer left to try and squeeze between barge and bank.

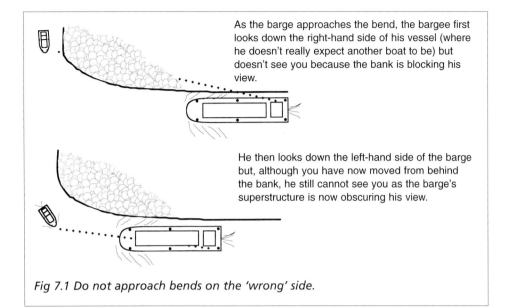

As the barge approaches the bend, the bargee first looks down the right-hand side of his vessel (where he doesn't really expect another boat to be) but doesn't see you because the bank is blocking his view.

He then looks down the left-hand side of the barge but, although you have now moved from behind the bank, he still cannot see you as the barge's superstructure is now obscuring his view.

Fig 7.1 Do not approach bends on the 'wrong' side.

Whichever you chose, the appropriate sound signal might help to avoid collision.

On the Continent, small craft do not use sound signals when meeting commercial vessels or other small craft. In the UK, a sound signal of two short blasts may be given by pleasure cruisers wishing to pass starboard to starboard.

Meeting in narrow channels

On the Continent, you are unlikely to come across a channel so narrow (except one controlled by traffic lights) that a pleasure boat could not pass a vessel coming the other way. Nevertheless, you should go through a narrow channel as quickly as is prudently possible and, if your view is restricted, you should also sound one long blast before entering the section, and periodically repeat it if the section is long. Do not repeat the blast continuously – for that is a distress signal.

Small craft must always give way to other vessels which are approaching or passing through a narrow channel. However, if you are going upstream and can see that a small craft bound downstream is approaching the narrow channel you should wait until it has passed. If you are going downstream and see that a small craft coming upstream has already entered the channel, wait until it has passed.

Where upstream and downstream are not defined, the following CEVNI rule applies: vessels with no obstacle to starboard, and those with the outside of a curved channel to starboard, should hold their course. Other vessels should wait until they have passed (Fig 7.2). Although CEVNI does not apply in the UK, it is a good practice to follow that rule anyway.

If you meet another boat in a narrow channel, do everything possible to pass with the minimum of danger (eg stop, squeeze into the side). If you think a collision is likely, sound a series of very short blasts.

Narrow channels are often controlled by traffic lights and/or signs, eg no passing or overtaking sign. The mandatory 'Pay attention' sign may be used to give advance warning signals/signs prohibiting passage (Fig 7.3).

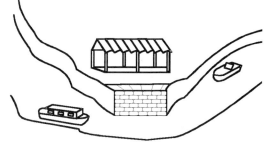

Overtaking

Sooner or later, you are going to catch up a slower boat and will want to overtake. Whatever the cir cumstances, the boat that is being overtaken has priority and it is your responsibility to make sure you can overtake safely. Never overtake near locks, tunnels and bridges, or where you see one of the signs in Fig 7.4.

Fig 7.2 The sports boat should give way to the narrow boat.

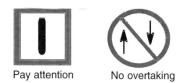

Pay attention   No overtaking

Fig 7.3 Mandatory signs.

In most parts of the UK you always overtake down the port side of the other vessel, but on the Continent you may also overtake on the starboard side provided the waterway is, unquestionably, wide enough.

Getting stuck behind a slow-moving barge on a very small continental water-

---

The red-bordered sign, with red diagonal, which is often displayed at the entrances to narrow channels, means 'no passing or overtaking'.

This sign permits passing but forbids any vessel to overtake another. This sign forbids a convoy to overtake another convoy, except when one is a pushed convoy of less than 110 metres long and 12 metres wide.

Fig 7.4 Signs prohibiting overtaking.

way can be frustrating. The bargee is under no obligation to slow down or move over to let you by, but that doesn't mean that he won't do so voluntarily. Ease to each side in turn and take a good look, to make sure there is no oncoming traffic. Then move closer and watch for a slight alteration in the barge's course to leave more room, or a hand waved in a 'come on' gesture. If getting closer reveals mud swirling in the water, kicked up by the barge's bottom, you can be sure that the bargee won't risk moving to the side for the convenience of a *plaisancier*, so you'll have to resign yourself to staying behind.

Popular touristic canals can be chaotic in high season.

You must stay behind if the vessel in front emits five short blasts. This signal means, 'You can't overtake me'. Heed it, even if you can't see any reason not to pass; the bargee may know something you don't about water depth near the banks. Drop back and follow at a safe distance, because sooner or later the barge will slow down and pull alongside a factory quay and he will then need room to manoeuvre.

Although pleasure craft do not normally give sound signals when overtaking, you must always take any necessary action to avoid danger. So if you are in the process of overtaking a barge and it alters course towards you, give the appropriate sound signal to let him know where you are. Two long blasts followed by two short ones if you are overtaking to port, two long blasts followed by one short one if you are overtaking to starboard.

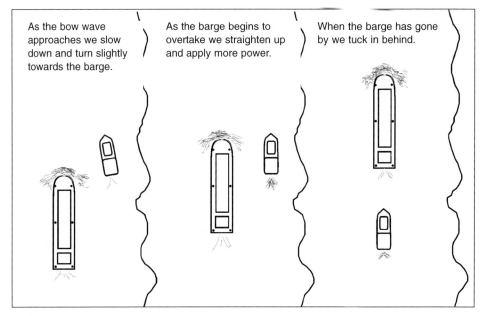

As the bow wave approaches we slow down and turn slightly towards the barge.

As the barge begins to overtake we straighten up and apply more power.

When the barge has gone by we tuck in behind.

Fig 7.5 Being overtaken.

Being overtaken

You are, in fact, much more likely to be overtaken by a commercial vessel than to overtake one. A lot has been written about suction drawing vessels together, but we've found that, whenever we have been overtaken by a barge, any suction effect has been more than counteracted by the effect of the bow wave pushing our boat away. One day, as a barge began to overtake, we were lifted up and carried several metres towards the bank. When the barge had passed, the water drained back, leaving us firmly held by glutinous mud. We gave one long horn blast, meaning 'Attention!', and, as a head popped out of the wheelhouse of the barge, followed up with four short blasts to say, 'We cannot manoeuvre.' Soon the barge was back, this time arriving more decorously, and we were towed off. To avoid a repetition of this incident, we now use the technique illustrated in Fig 7.5 when being passed, or overtaken, in confined waters.

Avoiding the bottom

The possibility of going aground is often a worry when cruising small canals and rivers and, because of their size, relative to the space available for manoeuvres, narrow boats are particularly vulnerable. The vast majority of canals, and dug sections of canalised rivers, have sloping sides. On some small canals, silt build-ups (between side and bottom) could be sufficient to ground a boat that was motoring close to the side. Similar situations can arise

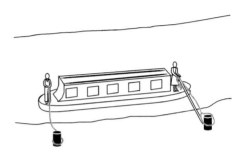

Fig 7.6 Using the mooring loop and special boathook.

in river sections with natural banks. If you get stuck in this way, the boat will probably be hard on and heeled. You may release it by getting several people to stand on the side furthest from the bank, whilst others pole off. Synchronised jumping up and down, to rock the boat, can also help. If that doesn't work and you can't get a tow off, you are faced with getting someone ashore. They could have a long walk to the nearest bridge, and back down the other side, before they can catch a rope and pull – which means that even narrow boats need dinghies!

Boats are in similar danger of grounding when approaching moorings. For example, when you are approaching a canalside pontoon, it seems easier to keep your boat near the bank and almost parallel to it so that you can edge gently alongside. However, using that technique, you could easily get stuck as silt tends to build up at the extremities of bankside structures. To minimise grounding risks you should approach pontoons, quays and banks, very slowly, at a pronounced

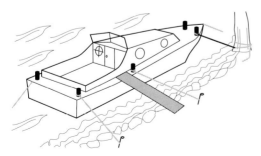

Fig 7.7 Mooring near to a rocky bank.

angle with someone watching out on the bow. The lookout should have bow and stern ropes with them (or bow and centre ropes if the boat is very long), and should pass them under any rails/wires before stepping off. If you do go aground whilst slowly approaching at an angle, you should only have your bows on and will, probably, be able to reverse off.

When you are in doubt about

bankside water depth, and conditions make it difficult to approach at much of an angle, you can use the following technique (provided there are bollards). Stop your boat parallel to the bank, but some distance from it, and use your special boathook to put lines on to the bollards (Fig 7.6). Then pull the boat in very gently. Stop hauling, of course, if you feel extra resistance, or see mud swirling up. This technique is especially useful when mooring narrow boats in less well-maintained waterways.

When you have to moor, but suspect that rocks lurk underwater, stop parallel to the bank, but just off it, and drop front and stern anchors. From near the front of the boat, push out a boathook or ladder (it must be the latter in rough water or windy conditions). When one end is on the bank, tie the other end to the boat. Do the same thing from near the back of the boat, with the boarding plank. You can then go ashore to secure the ends that are on the bank and, if necessary, fasten lines to mooring spikes (Fig 7.7).

Leaving a mooring

When leaving a mooring in a narrow boat there is a risk of damaging the rudder on the canal side. The easiest way to avoid this is to pole off sideways, parallel to the bank. If you are short on manpower, keep the bow rope on, release the stern and pole off at the back. When the stern is well clear of the side, release the bow, pole off and drive forward, using as little throttle as possible. Leaving a mooring in a conventional cruiser is usually less of a problem. We leave at the same sharp angle as we approach, to ensure that we avoid any obstructions on the exit, and station someone on the stern who is ready to fend off if the back swings in. The risk of going aground is greatest in droughts but, in those conditions, damage from underwater obstructions is less likely. Chunks of concrete, broken from canal sides, and other debris are easily seen when levels are low. When the level is that bit higher, murky water can conceal potential bottom rippers. We once read something like 'Km 50. Quay right bank' in a canal guide. We wanted to stop, so seeing a brick wall, at 50 kilometres, we headed for it, only to find that the quay had long disintegrated, leaving dangerous spikes jutting from the bottom. We were lucky to spot them and, since then, have been especially vigilant when near canal or river banks.

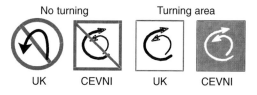

No turning · Turning area
UK · CEVNI · UK · CEVNI

Fig 7.8 Turning.

Turning

Never turn your boat if doing so would force another boat to make a sudden course or speed alteration and always pay special attention when approaching recommended turning areas. You must not turn where the CEVNI 'No turning' sign is displayed (Fig 7.8).

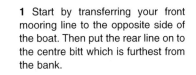

1 Start by transferring your front mooring line to the opposite side of the boat. Then put the rear line on to the centre bitt which is furthest from the bank.

2 One person starts the swing by poling off the stern with the boathook, gradually coming towards the front of the boat as it swings out. The other person pulls on the front rope.

3 When the boat has reached an angle of 45° to the bank, the person using the boathook takes the front rope and pulls as shown. The other person picks up the centre rope and pulls as shown. Once the boat has gone through a right angle, the rest of the manoeuvre requires little effort, unless there is a strong off-shore wind.

Fig 7.9 Even if you have one of the longer narrow boats, you can turn it without ultra long warps.

When we have nosed into a shallow backwater for a peaceful night's sleep, we often turn the boat on ropes. It greatly reduces the chances of getting stuck and is often quicker than shunting to and fro with the engine – especially with a narrow boat. It's also more environmentally friendly! (See Fig 7.9.)

Moving bridges

On small canals and rivers, swing bridges and lifting bridges come in DIY, semi-automatic or manned versions.

There is considerable variety in bridge types, but basic rules and procedures apply to all. Never try to put the operator directly on to the bridge; land

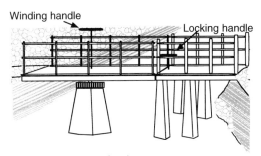

Fig 7.10 Rotating bridge.

Winding handle

Locking handle

When this swing bridge on the Canal du Centre, Belgium opens, the operator loses contact with land.

them before you get there. Also, it is important not to moor a narrow boat too near to the gap you are going to pass through (known as a 'bridge hole' in the UK). The person you put ashore must be strong enough to get a swing bridge going, or heavy enough to keep a lift bridge open – you don't want it to descend on the cabin top as you are passing. If the bridge is on a vehicular road, make sure that no traffic is approaching, then close the barriers. Some bridges have a safety mechanism that locks the bridge until barriers are down, then – once the bridge is moving – locks the barriers until it is closed again.

Many bridges need a key, or handle, to unlock them. On most UK waterways you should have your own. Elsewhere (and at some UK bridges) you can expect to find the key hanging near the bridge, or to get it from a nearby office. Be careful not to put the keys down, where they might end up in the water! Have a screwdriver with you in case you need to lever up a hatch that is covering a keyhole.

A common type of swing bridge turns against one bank. It is usually operated by pushing on a baulk of timber, and your strongest crew member may need help to persuade it to move! Once it is going you may have to restrain it from bouncing back at the end of the swing. Another type (Fig 7.10) opens into the middle of the canal, so once you've got it going you lose all contact with land. Although this type is operated by winding a mechanism, it can still be hard going – especially if it is a large bridge. Always read any instructions posted at moving bridges. Children should always remain on the boat (under the supervision of an adult) whilst crew members are opening swing bridges.

Many DIY lifting bridges are as basic as their swinging counterparts. You raise them by pulling a chain on the balance beam, then sit on the beam to keep them open. To close them, keep a hold on the chain, stand up, and gently lower the bridge.

On UK waterways, the hanging chain is sometimes replaced by a cable, attached to a winch drum, which can usually be turned by the key that you use to operate lock mechanisms. Others are operated

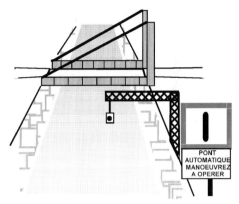

Fig 7.11 Automatic lifting bridge.

hydraulically, via electric circuits, and your key may unlock the control box. In other cases (and places), you may have to get a key from a nearby office. At mechanised lifting bridges, always read the instructions carefully and make sure you know about any devices that are used to retain the bridge in the open position. Modern bridges installed on roads that are fairly well frequented by vehicles, usually have chocks installed to minimise bouncing from crossing vehicles. Again, read the posted information about removing chocks and operating controls. Remember to replace chocks after your boat has gone through, to avoid damage to the bridge. At all moving bridges, refasten any locks, or resecure any retaining chains, before leaving. Do not omit this when you see another vessel

A fixed bridge on the Canal du Centre, Belgium with a lifting bridge behind it.

approaching – it may stop, or turn round, before reaching the bridge.

On the Continent, semi-automatic bridges are not uncommon and you usually get advance warning that you are approaching one. The 'Attention' sign is displayed, often with an additional message about what you are expected to do (see Fig 7.11).

However, exactly just *what* you are supposed to do is not always clear! When we first saw the French sign in Fig 7.11 we thought we had to manoeuvre the boat about the canal in order to cross some sort of electric eye. In fact, we were supposed to get close to the bank and pull a lever, but by the time we realised that, we had already gone past. So, on the approach to an automatic lifting bridge, keep looking out (through binoculars) for the actuating mechanism.

In most parts of the Continent, moving bridges are manned, though not necessarily on a permanent basis. For example, current policy on smaller French rivers and canals is that if average daily barge traffic is between 1 and 3 vessels, several locks/bridges will be operated by one person, who will travel between them. If barge traffic is 4 to 20 vessels per day, bridges/locks will be automatic. If traffic exceeds 20 barges per day, bridges/locks will remain manually operated, with more staff. Other countries have similar policies.

Retaining manual operation when there is more commercial traffic is not as strange as it first seems. Automatic schemes need built-in safety factors, which cause delays. At automatic bridges, even when no vehicle is in sight, bells must ring, and lights flash for some time, to give warning that barriers are about to come down, whereas an operator would immediately lower them.

On stretches where one keeper operates several bridges/locks, you may encounter considerable delays. At the first lock, try to ascertain whether the operator will follow immediately. If commercial vessels are behind you, he will wait and let them through, before following what will have become a boat procession with you as its least important member. If a barge is coming the opposite way, he will wait for it before following you.

Don't worry if you come to a moving bridge and find no sign of life. If it's a 'one-man stretch', the operator at the last manned item will have made contact to say you are *en route*. In some regions, bridges are manned part time by someone living nearby, and you may see the sign that means 'Make a sound signal' – it's a solid black circle on a white background and there may be an additional panel, which tells you which signal to make. Even if there is no sign, try a long blast on the horn if you come to an unattended bridge, but don't keep repeating it until you make the locals angry.

Some bridges are operated by remote control from another bridge. We once approached a largish Dutch bridge with an impressive, but empty, control tower. When our horn produced no result, we attached the boat to a single pile. (A barge would have lain between two, but we were nowhere near long enough.) After some time spent yawing around in the gusting breeze, we abandoned that tactic and lay in the water, repeatedly drifting into shallows and poling out again.

Forty minutes later, we were bored with that, so decided to investigate the other bank with a view to getting ashore. As we edged in, the bridge opened and we then spotted the camera under the opening span, which was on the 'wrong' side of the river. The moral is, 'Keep your eyes open'!

Passing under bridges

No special technique is needed for passing through bridges, unless you are in a narrow boat on a small UK canal, where early English engineers tried to minimise costs by making spans as small as possible. The technique for passing head on through any narrow UK bridge, whether it is fixed, swing or lifting, is to look down one side of the boat and aim to clear that side of the bridge by about 9 inches (23 centimetres). In low wind conditions, slow down well before the bridge, then, as you get close, gently accelerate to give yourself more steerage control. If the wind is stronger your boat may be proceeding crabwise, in which case you will have to straighten it up just before you begin to accelerate through. This technique needs practice, so if you are not very experienced and the wind is strong, walk the boat through.

Larger fixed bridges should not present any problems, but you still need binoculars as you approach. Look out for signs that either recommend which arch you should use, or forbid you to go through a certain arch. Other signs may ask you to take certain actions, such as sounding your horn, and there may be buoys marking obstructions at the water's edge. There will almost certainly be signs indicating air draft (very important if you are in a sailing vessel).

Tunnels

Essentially, a tunnel is a narrow channel with a roof, and an aqueduct is a high narrow channel. Some UK tunnels and aqueducts have traffic lights; others have notices about recommended practice near the entrance. On the Continent, most have traffic lights that are operated from nearby locks, but a few have some sort of lever/button, near the entrance, that you have to pull/press to make sure the lights at the other end turn red. Tunnels through which you are towed will be covered later (see page 95).

Speed limits

Most canals and rivers have speed limits; usually the smaller they are, the lower the limit (less than 4 mph in most of the UK). Of course, logs

Fig 7.12 Do not create wash.

are vulnerable to fouling by weed, so many inland waterway boats don't have one (at least, not one that works). If you don't have a log, try to get the feel of your boat at various speeds, by timing your vessel over a known distance.

On most continental waterways, half kilometre posts make this easy, especially if your engine has a rev counter. In the UK, you could time yourself between locks or bridges. Try setting the throttle to, say, 1000 rpm, and then seeing how long it takes to cover 1 kilometre, or 1 mile, in the stillest water you can find. Then repeat the exercise at other engine revolutions. Of course, none of that takes into account current, wind etc, and in fact there are times when keeping to the speed limit is nigh impossible. One day we slogged up the Waal at 5 kph, turned into the Pannerdens Canal to the Gelderse IJssel and found ourselves bounding along at 17 kph with the engine barely ticking over.

Whatever the speed limit, never go so fast that you create a big bow wave, turbulent wake or breakers on the shore. Never create wash when passing boats displaying 'No wash' signals and when the sign shown in Fig 7.12 is on the bank.

You must always avoid creating excessive wash, or suction, that might damage vessels or structures. In particular, you should reduce speed, providing you can do so without affecting your ability to steer your boat, when you are outside harbour entrances or near to moored vessels or ferry boats which are not moving independently. Large vessels are not obliged to take precautions to reduce speed in order to limit wash or suction when passing moored small craft. However, on the smaller waterways you will find that *péniches* often slow down when passing moored pleasure craft.

Warning and distress signals

If you go aground or break down, you should warn approaching boats by swinging a red flag by day. At night, or if the visibility is poor, a light should be used instead of the flag. Vessels normally use a red lamp, but small craft may use a white one. The flag or lamp is waved through a half circle.

If a red flag or light is swung through a full circle, it indicates that the vessel is in distress. Another distress signal is to repeatedly and slowly raise and lower the arms. Alternative distress signals are repeated long horn or whistle blasts sending SOS in Morse code, flares emitting stars and burning oily waste to create flames and smoke (see Appendix A).

If you see any of these signals from another boat, you must do everything you can to help, with the proviso that you must not put your own boat, or crew, at risk.

8

Buoys, landmarks and waterway rules

Upstream, downstream

The rule we mentioned earlier on page 74 about downstream vessels having priority, needs a bit of clarification. In flowing rivers, it is obvious which vessels are going downstream. In other cases, the authorities stipulate which vessels are classed as going downstream, but there are some recognised principles about this.

River trade is one of the oldest forms of transport, but as the system and the boats got bigger, original watercourses were often inadequate. Channels were dredged, banks cut back and rivers were 'canalised', ie made more suitable for navigation by means of locks, barrages etc. In some places settlements had sprung up at strategic river crossings and these had grown into towns, with buildings lining both banks, so enlargement of the river was impracticable. In other regions, the nature of the terrain made it impossible to widen and deepen a river. In those cases, bypasses, known as 'lateral canals', were constructed. The downstream vessel on a lateral canal is the vessel that would be going downstream if using the original river route.

To get vessels from one river to another, link canals were built. On these, the downstream vessel is the one that is descending the locks. If the link canal has no locks and is in the summit level (the lockless stretch on the top of a hill) of those that do, there are specific local definitions. Earlier we said that pleasure boats must keep to the right. That means you must be nearest to the bank on your right, which isn't the same as 'you must keep to the right bank'. Before I took up inland waterway cruising, I was confused when I saw signs in French towns saying, 'Rive droite' or 'Rive gauche'. 'Surely,' I would say to myself, 'whether it's the right bank or the left bank must depend on which way I'm facing?' Not so; the right bank is the bank that is on your right when you are travelling downstream. That same bank is still the right bank when you are going upstream, even though it will then be on your left!

Buoys

This question of right and left brings us to the subject of the inland waterway buoyage system. When you are going with the current, ie when the right bank is

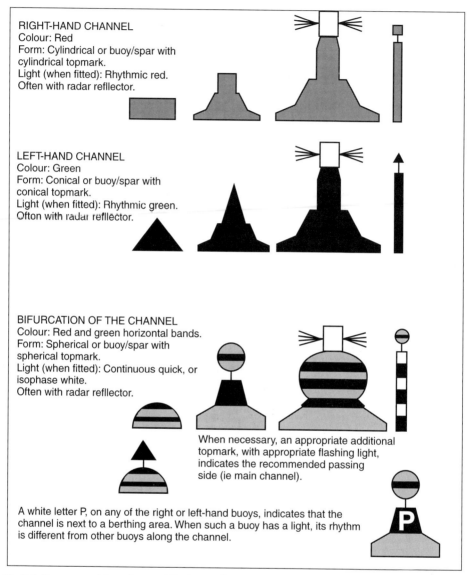

RIGHT-HAND CHANNEL
Colour: Red
Form: Cylindrical or buoy/spar with cylindrical topmark.
Light (when fitted): Rhythmic red.
Often with radar refllector.

LEFT-HAND CHANNEL
Colour: Green
Form: Conical or buoy/spar with conical topmark.
Light (when fitted): Rhythmic green.
Ofton with radar refllector.

BIFURCATION OF THE CHANNEL
Colour: Red and green horizontal bands.
Form: Spherical or buoy/spar with spherical topmark.
Light (when fitted): Continuous quick, or isophase white.
Often with radar refllector.

When necessary, an appropriate additional topmark, with appropriate flashing light, indicates the recommended passing side (ie main channel).

A white letter P, on any of the right or left-hand buoys, indicates that the channel is next to a berthing area. When such a buoy has a light, its rhythm is different from other buoys along the channel.

Fig 8.1 Buoys marking channel limits in the waterway.

on your right, the buoys on your right will be red, or predominantly red. When you are going against the current, the buoys on your right will be green, or predominantly green. In some countries black may be used instead of green, and on some heavily wooded Scandinavian waterways, green is replaced by white to make buoy spotting easier.

On some large expanses of water, like Friesland's meers, local decisions about which is deemed to be upstream and downstream on the channels entering the meers can cause confusion. Some of the larger meers are criss-crossed by a number of buoyed channels, which lead to inland creeks. You need to study your map carefully to make sure that you know which buoys you need to follow, and you need to be vigilant to avoid heading somewhere you don't want to go! In regions where all surrounding land is flat, the view can be confusing, especially at sunset.

Buoy shapes and colours are not easy to make out at sunset.

The pleasure boat in Fig 8.2 wants to enter a channel that lies almost directly ahead, but the buoys leading to it are difficult to distinguish. A steersman who has not studied his map would not know that the relative positions of the red and green buoys in the channel he is aiming for are not the same as those leading from the channel by the windmill. He might mistakenly head for the wrong channel, keeping the red buoys on his right, and end up aground! Looking through binoculars would show the changeover of the buoys, with the red and green bifurcation buoy marking the point where the channels divide.

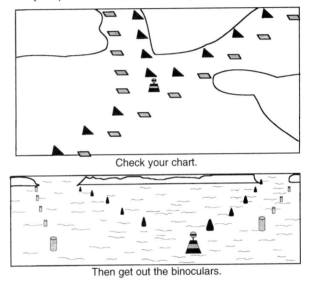
Check your chart.

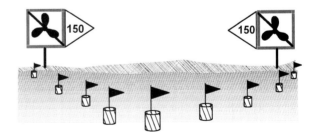
Then get out the binoculars.

Fig 8.2 Identifying buoys.

Yellow buoys

Cylindrical yellow buoys may be used to mark 'No Go' areas. On large expanses

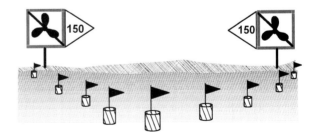

Fig 8.3 No motorised vessels.

of water, these often mark areas reserved for a particular activity. Sometimes they carry symbols, such as a white water skier on a blue background, to indicate the purpose that the area is reserved for. Sometimes yellow buoys are mounted with red flags and there may be other associated signs on the bank. In Fig 8.3 motorised vessels are banned from this area.

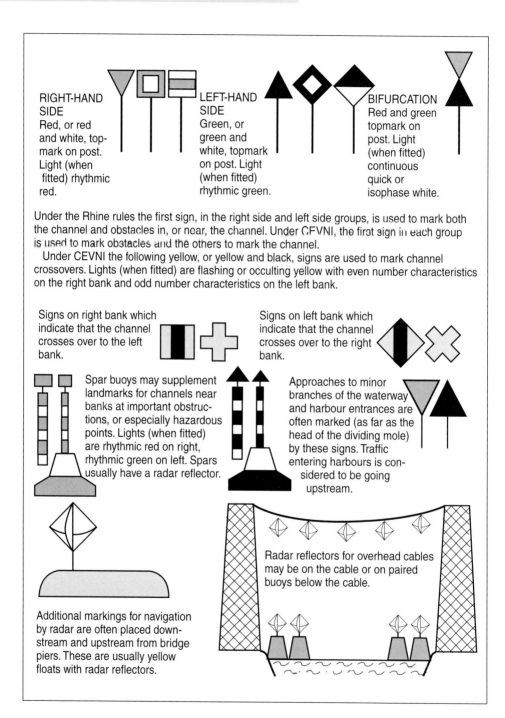

RIGHT-HAND SIDE
Red, or red and white, top-mark on post. Light (when fitted) rhythmic red.

LEFT-HAND SIDE
Green, or green and white, topmark on post. Light (when fitted) rhythmic green.

BIFURCATION
Red and green topmark on post. Light (when fitted) continuous quick or isophase white.

Under the Rhine rules the first sign, in the right side and left side groups, is used to mark both the channel and obstacles in, or near, the channel. Under CEVNI, the first sign in each group is used to mark obstacles and the others to mark the channel.

Under CEVNI the following yellow, or yellow and black, signs are used to mark channel crossovers. Lights (when fitted) are flashing or occulting yellow with even number characteristics on the right bank and odd number characteristics on the left bank.

Signs on right bank which indicate that the channel crosses over to the left bank.

Signs on left bank which indicate that the channel crosses over to the right bank.

Spar buoys may supplement landmarks for channels near banks at important obstructions, or especially hazardous points. Lights (when fitted) are rhythmic red on right, rhythmic green on left. Spars usually have a radar reflector.

Approaches to minor branches of the waterway and harbour entrances are often marked (as far as the head of the dividing mole) by these signs. Traffic entering harbours is considered to be going upstream.

Radar reflectors for overhead cables may be on the cable or on paired buoys below the cable.

Additional markings for navigation by radar are often placed downstream and upstream from bridge piers. These are usually yellow floats with radar reflectors.

Fig 8.4 Landmarks used to mark the channel near the bank.

Landmarks and other channel markings

As well as the buoys described above, landmarks are often used to mark channels near banks and yellow and black signs are used to mark crossovers.

In rural and little frequented areas, some rather 'homespun' methods may be used to mark channels. The humble withy is used: when the branches point upwards, the withy marks the right side of the channel; when the branches are tied so that they point down, the withy marks the left side. In Friesland and on some Italian rivers, we've also seen slatted wooden cones marking channels.

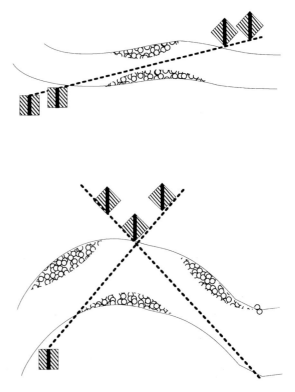

Crossing the path of other vessels

Fig 8.5 These drawings show you how to avoid shallow areas by lining up crossover marks.

On large expanses of water there are rules about crossing the path of other vessels. These rules are very similar to the *International Regulations for the Prevention of Collisions at Sea* that any reader who has crossed the Channel should be familiar with. Before we give the rules, there are some fundamental principles that you should always keep in mind.

Understanding priorities

When vessels of different types are in sight of each other, CEVNI – like *IRPCS* – normally awards priority to the least manoeuvrable vessel. This is why the Code does not differentiate between 'pleasure boats' and 'commercial vessels', but between 'small craft' and 'normal vessels'. So, the first thing to remember is that, unless you are steering a converted barge, or a luxury 20+ metre yacht, everything over 20 metres has priority over you.

The other thing to remember is that, regardless of anything in the following Rules of the Road, if you are following the starboard side of a marked channel and are in sight of another small craft that would normally have priority over you, you maintain your course and speed and the other vessel gives way.

Rules of the Road

- When two vessels are crossing in such a manner that there is a risk of collision, the vessel that has the other vessel to starboard gives way and, if possible, avoids crossing ahead of it.
- The same rule applies when one motorised small craft crosses the path of another, but when a large vessel crosses the path of a small craft, it maintains its course and speed, unless by doing so it would put the small craft in danger. Similarly, a small craft with priority over another small craft, must, if necessary, slow down or alter course to avoid endangering the other vessel.
- Motorised small craft give way to non-motorised small craft, and small craft that are neither motoring nor under sail give way to small craft under sail.
- When two small sailing craft are on a potential collision course and on a different tack, the one with the wind to port gives way.
- When two sailing craft are on a potential collision course and on the same tack, the vessel to windward gives way.
- If you are in a sailing craft with the wind on your port side, and you see another sailing craft on a potential collision course to windward but cannot determine which tack the craft is on, you must give way.
- When a small sailing craft is overtaking another, the overtaking craft should pass on the side on which the overtaken craft has the wind.
- When another category of small craft is being overtaken by a small sailing craft, it should, if necessary and safe to do so, manoeuvre to allow the overtaking to take place on the side on which the overtaking craft has the wind.

Lock technology

In the eighteenth century, staircase locks (see page 102) were one of the main barriers to efficient movement of goods. Various strategies were used to minimise the problems, such as stacking barges (one in each lock) and having specific ascending and descending days. Even so, delays were often long and frequent, especially when there was little difference between a laden barge's draft and the normal water depth. In that era, the techniques and machinery needed to make and operate a deep lock did not exist, so engineers began to think of alternative solutions.

Inclined planes

In 1789 William Reynolds invented his inclined plane and installed it on the Ketley Canal. Essentially, trolleys were installed in locks, built at the end of each level. Boats entered the locks and water was pumped out so that they settled on the trolleys. The gates were then opened and the descending trolley plus barge ran down railway lines, pulling the ascending one up. The drawback of this simple system was that the interchange could only take place when the descending barge was full and the ascending one less than 30 per cent full. This was not a problem at Ketley and on other canals where most cargoes were going downstream, but in other cases the interchange had to be assisted by steam, water or power. Planes of this type have now all but disappeared; however, one is still fully operational on the Elblasko-Ostrodzki Canal in Poland.

This early form of inclined plane soon gave way to a more advanced version, in which boats went into upper and lower spur canals and entered enclosed basins. Additional water was admitted to the upper basin, which then descended and dragged the lower basin up. Modern versions of this type are still in use, one of the largest being the 1432 metre-long Ronquières lift in Belgium, which can move a 1350 ton barge through a 68 metre level change.

Boat lifts

Boat lifts work on a similar principle, but raise and lower vessels vertically. The UK's Anderton lift is a well-known tourist attraction, and many Mediterranean bound boaters pause to marvel at the equally famous *ascenseur* at Fontinettes. Fontinettes is now defunct, but in the recently restored Anderton and on Belgium's Canal du Centre you can still experience the unique sensation of being almost 15 metres above the canal, with just a metre or so showing on your echo sounder.

Entering an inclined plane or lift basin is little different from entering a lock. They are controlled by traffic lights and, when you get a green light, you simply steer the boat into a basin and tie up to one of many convenient bollards. You really can tie up, because your boat's position is not going to vary relative to the water it is floating in. Your work load during the ride is nil, except to make sure that children are in a safe place.

Circular locks

So far we've given the impression that locks are always oblong boxes, but this isn't so. Every now and then one encounters a more strangely shaped lock, and there are even completely circular ones. At locks like these you obviously cannot use any of the standard techniques; however, they do not normally present problems. One of two situations usually apply: out of the holiday season you have plenty of manoeuvring room and can pick a mooring place at leisure; during holiday periods, these locks can get very crowded and often the keeper, or his assistant, will direct you to a spot and take your lines. In some places, these locks are only operated during certain specific periods of the day, so you can have quite a wait – and a possible rearrangement of everyone's moorings each time another vessel comes along.

Weirs

At times, some locks are used to let excess water out of canals and rivers, and on these occasions local signs may be used to let boats know what is happening. For example, at Nieuwpoort, red balls are hoisted when any of the locks are draining excess water into the sea. If you don't understand a particular signal displayed at a lock, steer clear until you've found out what it means.

Weirs have been a river feature for centuries. Most of the early ones were built by millers who wanted to ensure that they had an adequate supply of water. When rivers were navigable, gates were fitted at the centre of the weir so that boats could be passed through. Downstream vessels went through on the water passing down when the gates were opened; upstream vessels had to wait for the lower level to be raised enough for the boat to be dragged over the weir. Letting water through was called 'getting a flash', so the passages got the name 'flash locks'. Few still exist; I know of none in use, but weirs still abound and must be treated with great caution.

British Waterways excels in the precautions it takes to minimise the chances of you accidentally taking your boat too close to a weir. Many (though not all) are situated in a biggish loop (bypassing a lock), with the route to the lock and the 'no go' branch clearly indicated by the main road-style signs (described in Chapter 6), sited well before the junction. A little further on, channel buoys and direction arrows confirm the route to be taken. Even so, the view from a boat can be confusing, with low lying land merging into water and the actual weir almost indiscernible (Fig 9.1).

Through binoculars, swirling water and a protective boom show up the weir.

The details on the main sign, the additional arrows pointing to the lock and the state of the lock can all be picked out.

In many parts of the Continent, weirs are by no means so clearly marked. This is one of the reasons that not bothering to buy a detailed map, on the grounds that you can't get lost going straight down a river, is very unwise. Never assume that weirs will be signposted; we

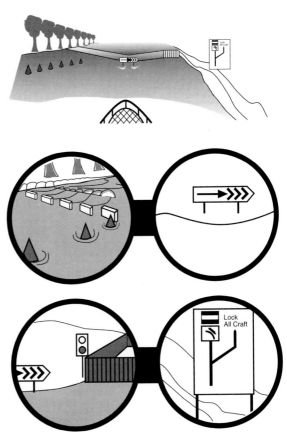

Fig 9.1 Top: With the naked, eye neither weir nor lock entrance can be clearly seen. Centre and below: Binoculars enable you to clearly make out direction signs, weir boom and lock.

have encountered many locks with a weir at the side, and little, or nothing, to indicate its presence. When travelling downstream, these side weirs in the main flow are not at all easy to spot, so a map is absolutely essential. Whenever your map indicates that you are nearing a weir, get out the binoculars and ascertain exactly where it is and which course you must steer to avoid getting close. In some Scandinavian canals, for example, the fact that there is a weir in a loop round a lock may not be indicated. There may only be an arrow pointing in the direction you should take.

Commercial tunnels

Tunnels are almost always controlled by traffic lights and often there are advance warning lights. These usually comprise one or two white lights. When they are shining steadily you should stop, when they are isophase flashing you may proceed.

Before entering you should check your lights and have torches handy; don't let people stand up in tunnels and watch out for overhead electric cables.

Vessels are towed through some tunnels and the usual order of the tow is laden commercials, unladen commercials, pleasure craft – with the smallest at the back. If you are the only vessel being towed, the lines will usually be supplied by the tug. Otherwise, attach yourself to the boat in front, using your two longest lines – left stern bitt of front vessel to your right forward bitt and right stern bitt of front vessel to your left forward bitt. The longer the tow, the more control you will have, so if necessary, join some lines together – 30 metres is probably optimum but this would depend on tunnel bends, so ask the staff. You can at the same time ask whether there are any local regulations concerning action during emergencies, eg a tow parting.

Strictly according to the rules, you should not use your engine when being towed through, but you may have difficulty steering your boat at the slow tow speed. It is a good idea to tell staff that you have trouble keeping straight when under tow, and request permission to keep the engine ticking over. In some tunnels staff actively encourage pleasure craft users to do this, as they do not want you to have an encounter with the tunnel walls (see also Tunnels, page 85).

Small lock techniques 10

A lock is an oblong basin, with gates at each end to allow boats to enter and exit. By letting water into it, or draining it out, boats go up and down. Water is let into, or out of, the lock by means of sluices (called 'paddles' in the UK). These may be gate sluices, or ground sluices, or both. Below the upper lock gates, a cill extends into the lock. It can only be seen when the lock is empty.

'Empty' locks are not really empty. The word is used to describe a lock that is ready to accept a boat from the lower level, or let one out to that level. Similarly, 'full' locks do not have water brimming at the top of the walls. The water level in a full lock is the same as that in the upper section of the canal or river.

Sluice types

Very old locks had, and often still have, only gate paddles, which are simply oblong covers over slots in the gates. The disadvantage of this type (especially when a boat is going up) is that it creates a mini waterfall that causes considerable turbulence, and it has even been known to sink a boat that is imprudently positioned too near the upper gates! Locks of this type are common in Sweden and Norway, where the view from the boat, when going up, can be quite spectacular.

Ground paddles overcome the waterfall problem, and much of the turbulence, by letting water in via underground ducts. Quite often, locks have both ground and gate paddles, and this is the type you will frequently encounter on UK canals.

Giant modern locks, with lifting gates that double as paddles, will be covered in Chapter 11, but you might see a more old-fashioned version on small waterways. These are known as 'guillotine gates' and are rarely encountered at DIY canal locks. There are just two in the British Waterways network, and operating instructions are posted near the gates. However, lifting lower gates are quite common at manned river locks, such as those on the Nene.

Operating small locks

British Waterways are mechanising locks on more popular routes but, on the whole, gates at DIY locks in the UK are most likely to be opened by simply pushing on a beam that extends from the gate. On narrow UK canals there is usually

The wash from gate sluices can cause considerable turbulence.

one upper gate and two lower gates. On wider canals, upper and lower gates are usually paired. On the Continent, where even small locks are much bigger than their UK counterparts, there is usually some mechanical aid to the opening process.

Rack and pinion

Paddle-operating mechanisms also vary, but, overall, rack and pinion mechanisms are most often encountered. To use them you need a winding handle, often referred to as a lock key or even incorrectly described as a windlass. In the UK, when rack and pinions are used to operate gate paddles, they are usually positioned on the gate opening beam and wound via a remote spindle.

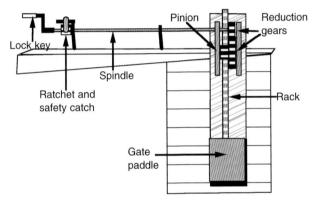

On the Continent, the spindle of the rack and pinion is often sited directly over the gate paddles, and you walk on to a small bridge to operate the mechanism. Usually there are high and low gear options, with high gear faster but harder work. Operating mechanisms for ground paddles are situated on the lock quay, near the gates. However, in some regions gate paddles are also operated from quay-mounted equipment, so do not assume that a mechanism on the quay will necessarily be operating a ground paddle.

Fig 10.1 Rack and pinion lock mechanism.

All paddles should be lowered in a controlled manner, eg wound down, when using a rack and pinion mechanism. Simply dropping paddles may damage them, and if you have forgotten to remove the winding handle, this could fly off and injure someone.

DIY locks

Knowing which type of paddles are installed will help DIY operators to give the boat a comfortable passage, especially when ascending, by opening them in the correct sequence. The series of four drawings in Figs 10.2 to 10.5 shows the sequence of operating locks, for ascents and descents, plus the sequence for opening paddles during an ascent. Following this sequence, and opening paddles slowly, will minimise turbulence.

Figs 10.2–10.5 show one boat in a wide lock. When two boats are opposite each other in a wide lock, the paddles should be opened slowly and simultane-

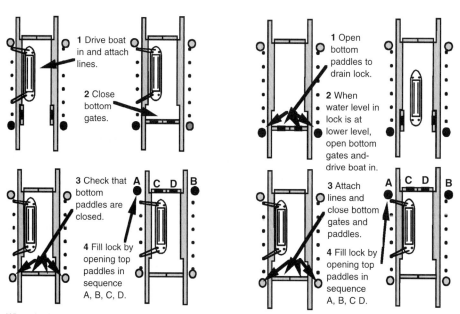

When the water level in the lock is the same as the upper level, open the top gates and drive the boat out. Close the top gates and the paddles behind you, if that is the regional custom.

Fig 10.2 Going up – lock empty. Open the bottom gates (if not already open).

Fig 10.3 Going up – lock full. Check that the top gates and paddles are closed.

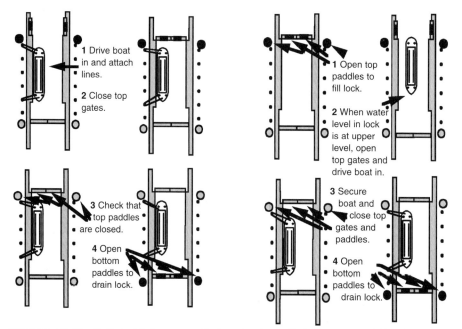

When the water level in the lock is the same as the lower level, open the bottom gates and drive the boat out. Close the bottom gates and the paddles behind you, if that is the regional custom.

Fig 10.4 Going down – lock full. Open the top gates (if not already open).

Fig 10.5 Going down – lock empty. Check that the bottom gates and paddles are closed.

ously by both operators. When descending in a lock with lower guillotine gates, the gate itself acts as the paddle. (This sequence will be shown in Chapter 11.)

Water conservation

During any lock cycle, the water used to fill or empty it is drained from the upper level. If the canal is to remain open for navigation, this water must be either recovered or replaced. Recovery involves directing water, drained from the lock, into a side pond, then pumping it back into the upper level. Replacing lost water is sometimes achieved by a natural flow from rivers, and sometimes by pumping from reservoirs. A standard-sized UK narrow boat lock, with a fall of 1 metre, would use about 50 cubic metres of water in its cycle and its Freycinet counterpart would use 200 cubic metres.

This water consumption has two implications for lock users. First, having seen the disturbance below the lower gates of a small emptying lock, you may be worried about the turbulence you might meet at bigger locks. However, don't be overly concerned, because when draining lock water directly into a canal or river would cause excessive turbulence, a proportion of the water will always be directed into a side pond. This not only virtually eliminates disturbance to boats, but it also avoids damage to banks and waterside buildings. For example, if the Fontinettes lock (cycle usage 21 000 cubic metres!) on the Dunkerque–Escaut waterway did not have a side pond, then the little town of Arques would be subjected to a mini-tidal wave each time vessels descended.

The second implication is that when operating DIY locks you should be conscious of the need to conserve water. Do not empty a lock so that you can ascend if a boat is approaching at the top level. Do not fill it if a boat is approaching at the bottom level. If you have passed another boat fairly near to a broad lock, or if you can see one coming up behind you, wait for that boat to arrive and share the lock.

Continental variations in lock procedure

In the UK operating a lock yourself is the normal procedure; however, in most parts of the Continent, it is a rare event. There are other differences between what you can expect to encounter at home and abroad. For a start, lock traffic lights are uncommon in the UK, but near-universal on the Continent. Also, it is normal practice (there are exceptions) to close UK lock gates behind you, whereas in many parts of the Continent the gates immediately behind an exiting boat are normally left open. So on the Continent you will often be able to go straight into a lock, but in the UK you will nearly always have to moor before the lock and walk up to open the gates, unless another vessel is coming through as you arrive. In the UK, you are expected to have your own handles for operating lock mechanisms. On the Continent, these are usually supplied to you at the last lock before the unmanned section, or are suspended near the mechanism.

Staircase locks

Today, single locks raise and lower vessels through level differences of many metres. In the past, large level differences were overcome by 'staircases' of linked locks, known as 'flights' in the UK, where the bottom gates of one lock are the top gates of another. In most parts of the Continent, lock flights are rarities and are usually only found on tourist canals in rural areas. In the UK and Scandinavia, they are quite common.

All Scandinavian staircases and the majority of UK examples are operated by keepers, at least during summer months, but you might have to work a flight yourself. There are two basic types: those where the water simply flows directly from one lock to another, and those where the water is routed via a side pond. The best-known side pond type is at Foxton, on the Leicester Canal, and the Bingley Five Rise is a famous example of the direct-feed type.

Working a staircase lock

Before you start to ascend, or descend, a staircase, you must first check that no boat is already inside, then prepare all the locks. Many boaters think that staircases are complicated, but – as long as you start off right – they are extremely simple. The thing to remember is that whether you are going up or down, top locks should always start off full and bottom locks should always start off empty. For the rest it is: GOING UP – MIDDLE LOCKS FULL; GOING DOWN – MIDDLE LOCKS EMPTY.

To go down a prepared staircase, open the top gates and drive the boat into the top lock. Close the gates behind your boat, then open the paddles, in and adjacent to the gates in front of it, so that the water drains from the top lock into the next one. When the levels are equal, close the paddles, open the gates, pass through to the next lock, and close the gates behind you. Repeat the procedure until you are at the bottom.

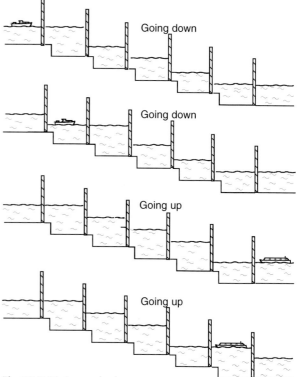

Fig 10.6 Staircase lock.

Going up is equally straightforward. After you have prepared the locks, open the lowest gates and drive your boat into the bottom lock. Close the gates behind your boat, then open the paddles in or adjacent to the gates in front of it, using the sequence that you would use for a single lock. When the levels are equal, close the paddles, open the gates and drive into the upper lock.

Who enters a lock first?

Large vessels take precedence at locks, just as they do everywhere else. Normally they will enter first, but there may be occasions when the lock keeper directs a small craft in first. Where there are only small craft waiting, and at DIY locks, it is good practice for steel boats to enter before solid wooden ones and for both to enter before GRP and plywood vessels. This minimises the risk of a strong heavy boat damaging a more vulnerable one. For the same reason, very small boats should go in last.

Passage through a lock

From the point of view of people on the boat, a lock passage can be divided into four stages: mooring before the lock (if necessary), approach and entry, securing inside, leaving. The actual techniques for pre-mooring are the same as those described in Chapter 11, but there are some factors to consider when choosing a mooring place.

When you first sight a commercial lock, get out the binoculars and look for lights or other clues as to the state of play. Green lights and open gates are the things you would like to see most, but, failing that, there could be other indications that soon things will, literally, be going your way.

If the lights are red and the gates are firmly shut, slow right down, keep watching the lock, and you may see the roof of a barge wheelhouse appear above the gates. In that case, by creeping forward very slowly you may avoid the need to go into the side and moor. We always like to avoid mooring at smaller locks, especially those in urban areas, because we have seen all sorts of underwater hazards near the banks.

Mooring outside the lock

If there is nothing going on at the lock to suggest that it will soon open for you, then there is no alternative but to moor, unless the wind and water are still and you have a controllable boat. Most bargees, for example, would simply let the vessel lie in the water, and correct any tendency to drift with occasional touches on throttle and rudder. If it becomes obvious that you must moor, don't forget to put someone on the bow to watch out for underwater hazards.

Narrow boats have to make precision entries to locks, so in this type of boat you must pick a mooring place that is far enough from the lock to enable you to get the boat pointing directly at the entrance, before the bow reaches the gates. If there is a wind blowing, try to moor where the wind will push you off from the bank when you are ready to leave. Otherwise, you could have difficulty getting away, especially if the vessel is undermanned. On small commercial canals, an exiting barge may have little room to manoeuvre, so don't station your boat too near. Pay particular attention to this when the lock is near a bend, or you could find a large black stern swinging uncomfortably close!

Approach and entry

A smooth passage through any lock starts with the approach, and when a lock is only a few inches wider than the boat, the correct approach is even more vital. So from the pleasure boating point of view, there is no doubt that the most difficult of all lock manoeuvres has to be the entrance of a narrow boat into one of the smaller UK locks. Aiming something that projects up to 21 metres in front of you into a hole that is only just a bit wider than that object takes a bit of practice. At least, doing it accurately does, especially if there's a strong wind blowing. On some UK canals you will have to do it many times, so before you go off on your first UK narrow canal jaunt, make sure you have a bit of practice under the watchful eye of an experienced narrow boat handler.

Of course, every year hundreds of people who have never steered boats in their lives, hire narrow boats and embark on holiday cruises. Those who hire smaller boats usually cope quite well but some – who have opted for a bigger boat and don't have enough crew members – have been known to spend a fortnight manhandling the vessel through every single lock.

There are times when manoeuvring a narrow boat by 'people power' is the easiest option, but it can be very tiring in heavily locked stretches; therefore it's a good idea to practise the right lock approach technique. This is basically the same as that used to pass through a bridge hole (see pages 80–4).

Cross-winds

If there is a strong cross-wind, the lock-operating person should go to a place near the entrance, where he can help if the boat gets swung round. The boat will have been motoring crab-wise, but the helmsman should have slowed down and straightened up on the approach to the lock, then gently accelerated to keep the boat straight. If the boat is still crab-wise when the front enters between the walls outside the gate, there will be virtually no wind force acting on the front section and the effect of the wind on the back will push the stern round. There are few narrow boat owners who can honestly say that they have never been in that situation, so, when the wind is strong, having ropes attached in readiness is a good idea. One should be on the front bitt, furthest from the wind. The other should be on the opposite side, attached to a bitt just aft of centre. Both ropes are then passed to the lock operator who secures the front line, in a way that will keep the bow in the centre of the lock gates. The other rope is then used to pull the stern in. As soon as the stern has been pulled in, the steersman steps off and temporarily secures the stern line. The lock operator crosses to the other side and catches the front line, thrown by the steersman. They are now in a position to pull the boat into the lock.

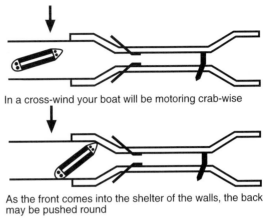

In a cross-wind your boat will be motoring crab-wise

As the front comes into the shelter of the walls, the back may be pushed round

In comparison to the narrow UK locks, the open gates of the wider ones will seem very inviting, and the smallest continental ones will look like the mouth of a gaping cavern. Even so, a smooth passage will still start with the approach. What you must not do is charge in as soon as the gate gap is wide enough for your boat.

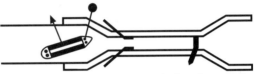

If you get into that position, secure the bow then use the second line to pull the stern in

Inside a lock

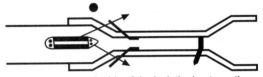

With a person on each side of the lock the boat can then be pulled in

Fig 10.7 Narrow boat entering a lock.

Anything written about boat handling usually includes lots of advice about mooring into wind, into tide etc, followed up by a whole host of diagrams showing what to do in a variety of circumstances when the ideal way is impossible, eg cross-winds and currents. This is all very sound advice, but it can't apply to handling a boat in a lock, where you have no choice but to secure your boat against that wall, regardless of the prevailing conditions. Also, until you actually enter a lock, you can't be sure what those conditions will be. A stiff breeze blowing down a waterway can 'wind tunnel' into a strong wind inside an empty lock, and when water levels are higher than desirable, paddles may be left open and can cause unexpected eddies. All this means that it is best to forget about advanced boat handling tactics and adopt a standard lock technique.

Standard continental lock technique for a cruiser

This standard technique will vary slightly, according to the type of boat you have, whether there is someone on shore to take lines, the depth of the lock, and whether you are going up or down. However, in all cases, there are two fundamental rules. Do everything slowly and secure the stern first. The first situation we are going to describe is a conventional cruiser, going down in a continental lock, with no one on shore to take the lines.

The helmsman should decide which wall of the lock he is going to moor against. As you will have been motoring on the right of the canal, you will normally moor on the right-hand side of the lock, but there may be a reason to choose the left, eg a boat is in front of you and is likely to go to the right. In a strong cross-wind, it is better to choose the wall where the wind will tend to push the boat on. Fending off is easier than trying to lassoo bollards when you are being blown off! When you have decided on the mooring side, put down fenders if you have no permanent protection system.

With a crew of two, the person who is to secure the boat should prepare the front rope first, by passing it under any rails or wires and walking back, with the looped rope, to just forward of the centre of the vessel. Leave the front rope there (making sure it cannot fall into the water) and prepare the rear rope in the same manner, coming back to where you left the front one. Loop the rear rope over your left arm and the front one over your right arm, and hold on to the grab rail whilst the boat enters the lock.

The helmsman should wait until the gates are fully opened and any exiting vessels have passed, then steer towards the lock, keeping as close to the selected wall as possible. The boat should be manoeuvred as slowly as possible and kept parallel to the lock side. The helmsman should take the decision about which mooring bollards to use, because he is the only person who can tell whether the boat can easily be stopped.

As the bow comes near his chosen bollard he calls, 'This one' (or any other equally nautical command you want to invent). The crew drops the *rear* rope over that bollard, then walks forward while paying it out. (If you put the front rope

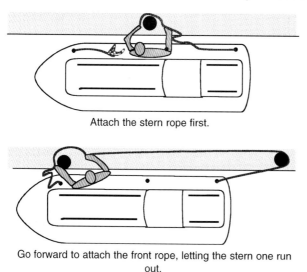

Attach the stern rope first.

Go forward to attach the front rope, letting the stern one run out.

Position the boat for the descent.

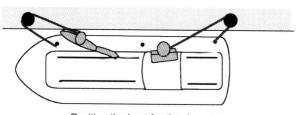

Fig 10.8 Attaching lines for descent.

on first, the stern will have a tendency to swing out.) The helmsman takes the boat out of forward gear, uses a touch of reverse throttle to slow the momentum, and then as the boat drifts slowly past another convenient bollard, the crew drops the front rope over it. The vessel is now loosely attached fore-and-aft and the helmsman can switch off the engine and join the crew in rope work and positioning the boat for the descent.

Narrow boat lock techniques

Once a narrow boat is inside a narrow lock, its crew has a decided advantage. With just a few centimetres on either side, the boat isn't going to go very far, other than backwards and forwards – and if it's a 70 footer, it isn't even going to do much of that! Also, as a member of the crew is going to operate the lock, you don't have to secure in any haste.

In a small narrow boat, with a crew of just two, the rope person prepares the front rope and leaves it in an easily picked-up loop, then goes to the back of the boat, prepares the rear rope and stands at the ready. When the helmsman says 'This one', the crew drops the rear rope, over the bollard and hands it to the helmsman. The crew then goes through the boat to the front, and drops the front rope over a bollard. With a longer boat, and three people, the helmsman does not need to be involved in rope handling.

Level changes

Small locks do not have big level changes. In many places, the difference between lower and upper level could be under a metre, so you will often be able to drop your lines over quayside bollards, even when going up. When ascending the deeper small locks, with bollards out of easy 'dropping-on' range, you use a slightly different technique: tie the end of a coil of rope, with a loop in the other end, to a front bitt and leave it at the front of the boat; attach a second rope, with a loop in one end, to a rear bitt and stand at the back of the boat, ready to lassoo a bollard, or to attach the rope with the special boathook. As soon as the rear rope is attached, shout 'ON' and go forward to attach the front line. The helmsman can now stop the boat and come on deck to look after the stern line, whilst you look after the front one.

Important note *This technique is only to be used when ascending in small locks. In large locks and when you are going to descend, you must never use loops over bollards, or tie your boat to the quay in any other way.*

When you will not secure your boat in a lock

There are two situations where you will not secure your boat in a lock. In certain popular UK and continental tourist areas, ropes are hung from lock sides and you simply hold on to these during the level change. In these cases, the rope person should take the rear line and hand it to the helmsman, before going forward to take the front rope. The other situation occurs only on some narrow UK locks, where no mooring bollards are provided. It is common practice, in this situation, for the steersman to keep the boat positioned by using the engine, but it is not something we would want to do (see below). As soon as we discovered that the locks on a particular waterway did not have bollards, we would (before reaching each lock) put sufficient people ashore to hold the boat.

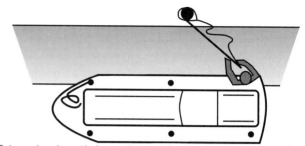

Going up in a deeper lock - use the special boathook to attach the stern line

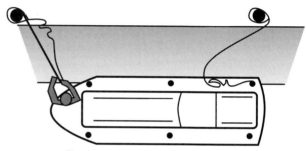

Then go forward and attach the front line loop

Fig 10.9 Attaching lines for ascent.

Avoid climbing ladders

Anyone who has previously read a book about inland waterway cruising will probably be wondering why we haven't mentioned the technique that seems to be almost universally described elsewhere, ie coming alongside a ladder so that someone can step off and shin up carrying the ropes. The reason is simple: we don't think it is a good idea because the rungs are invariably covered in a variety of substances, from algae to diesel oil, all of which are slippery. In our view, no one should attempt to get off a boat in a lock until the boat is secured.

We did some clambering in our early days, and rapidly decided that a ladder was the most likely place to have a canal accident, especially when hauling up two ropes. If you are asking yourself, 'Why should she be right and everyone else wrong?', note that, in thousands of kilometres of cruising the waterways of many countries, we have never seen any crew member, of any commercial vessel, go up a lock ladder to assist with mooring the vessel!

Do not run engines in locks

CEVNI states that engines should not be run in locks, though it has to be said that bargees do sometimes break the rule. Running an engine when not on the move unnecessarily pollutes the atmosphere, but the main reason for the ban is the danger of being maimed by a propeller. Even if your engine is out of gear, your propeller will probably be turning.

In the UK, many narrow boaters never secure (or only secure one rope) in narrow locks and use the engine to keep the boat where they want it, even where bollards are provided. I suppose their argument is that it is difficult to fall over the side of a locked-in narrow boat. However, you can fall off the back and someone could fall from the lock into the water behind the boat, so we do not think the practice can be recommended.

Your position in the lock

On the Continent, especially in Holland and Germany, the lock keeper may insist you lie in a certain place, even when you are alone in the lock. The reason for this usually remains a mystery. Given freedom of choice, a small boat and a lock that is roomy and free of other vessels, a position just behind the mid-point usually makes for the smoothest passage.

In a lock that only has gate paddles, make sure that, when ascending, you are not so far forward that the water pours into the front of the boat. Similarly, when waiting below a full lock with gate paddles, or with a guillotine gate, don't get too close or you could have a very bumpy time whilst the lock is emptying. If there are a lot of boats waiting to ascend a lock and you end up at the very back, look behind you for protuberances on the gates. There are often strengthening baulks of timber and it is easy to catch a narrow boat's tiller under one as the level rises. There is a similar problem if you are close to the front gates, where a pulpit could get caught under a timber. If either of these things should happen at a DIY lock, close the top paddles, then open a bottom paddle to allow water to drain out and release the boat. If it happens in a manned lock, yell.

Going down, you must be well forward of the upper gates, otherwise your stern gear could end up sitting on the cill and, almost inevitably, would be damaged. Sometimes white lines are painted on the lock wall, marking the cill position. In other cases, the pattern on the wall above the cill is different. If there are no clues to the cill position, the back of your boat should be at least 2 metres from the upper gates.

If you do get stuck on the cill, close the bottom paddles, then slightly open a top paddle and let in water until the vessel refloats. Check for any damage to your stern gear before you move on. First move the rudder full left and right. If you feel undue stiffness, or hear grating noises, haul the boat out of the lock on lines and phone for a tow. Next, visually examine the stern gland: excess water coming in would suggest a problem. If all is well so far, start the engine, select forward gear and move off with minimum throttle. If there are unpleasant noises or excessive vibration, switch off the engine and resort to ropes. If not, repeat the test in reverse and, if that seems OK, continue your journey, gradually increasing the engine revolutions until you are satisfied that all seems well. The possibility of accidentally landing on the rear cill is another very good reason for not running your engine in a lock. If a turning propeller makes contact with a cill, it will almost certainly be wrecked.

Keep that axe handy!

Provided that you remember never to tie up and make sure that no ropes can jam, you are not likely to get hung up on the wall during a descent. However, if this does happen you must cut the offending rope as quickly as possible. Use the axe, which will go through a taut rope much faster than a knife. If both ropes have tightened and you don't act quickly, the boat could tip sideways and someone could be thrown into the water. When just one end is fast, the danger is that the bitt to which the rope is attached could pull out, part of the deck could break away, or the rope could break. In either case, people could be thrown overboard when the vessel crashes down. Of course, whilst you are axing the rope, someone else should be sounding long blasts on your horn, shouting or radioing to the lock keeper, or getting someone to shut the bottom paddles if the lock is DIY.

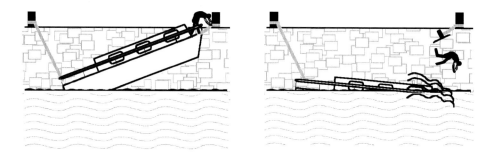

Fig 10.10 Axe quickly! Before you get to this stage.

Mechanised locks

You might imagine that boaters would welcome having the effort removed from lock operations, but there have actually been complaints when British Waterways have sawn off gate beams and installed mechanical opening devices! On the Continent, however, where most old locks were keeper operated, modernisation has been greeted with more enthusiasm.

In the UK, mechanised DIY locks are usually operated from the bank, so you still have to moor the boat so that someone can walk up to the lock. On the Continent, you operate the gate opening mechanism from your boat, by pulling a handle suspended over the waterway, or pushing a button mounted on a pile. As you enter the lock, you must keep looking out for the item that starts the cycle to let water in or out, because its position and type varies. The ones we encountered in our early days were all placed well inside the locks, so when we reached Dunkerque's lock on the Canal de Furnes, we sat mystified inside until someone chanced along and explained that these sluices were activated by something hanging by the gates.

The most common mechanism consists of a pair of buttons, green for start, red for emergency stop. They are sometimes mounted on a waterproof fitting, at the end of a flexible lead that lies on the lock quay. More often they are suspended over the lock or mounted on a pole. You can nearly always reach them from the boat but, as they are sited to be in a bargee's reach, it is possible that you will have to climb on to the quay to operate the mechanism. Obviously, you must not push or pull whilst other boats are entering or approaching the lock. When you have operated the mechanism, don't worry if nothing happens immediately! Automated locks have built-in delays for safety reasons, so they operate more slowly than their hand-operated counterparts.

The more modern type of semi-automatic lock is similar, but rather more sophisticated. One common system has an electric eye, which counts entering boats and displays the number on a digital counter. When the last one is inside, its crew repeatedly press a button until the displayed number is zero. There are even totally automatic locks, where you cross an electric eye on the approach, and everything else happens without you having to do a thing. Don't panic if you encounter one of this type; it will be set up to give you plenty of time to secure before water starts coming in or going out.

Leaving the lock

When the lock has completed its cycle, start the engine and leave it ticking over in neutral whilst you attend to the lines. If your boat is conveniently situated opposite two quayside bollards, you will be able to flick off the lines and unhurriedly motor out.

However, in commercial locks, bollards are rarely spaced for the convenience of *plaisanciers* so it's worth looking at a few do's and don't's.

Fig 10.11 shows a definite *don't*. If you simply start hauling in the stern line two things are likely to happen. First, the stern will probably swing out; secondly, the end is likely to trail in the water. There is often a flow, even in canal locks, because keepers sometimes open gates slightly in advance of getting a level, and a trailing rope could get caught up in a propeller.

The right way to let go is to pull on the rear line and pay out the front until the stern of the boat is opposite the back bollard. The steersman flicks the stern rope on to the deck, then returns to the controls and slowly drives the boat forward. As the bow approaches the front bollard, the crew flicks off the front line. Your actual departure from the lock wall should be carried out as slowly as possible and at the shallowest angle that will enable you to clear the gates. Too much throttle, or a sudden burst of throttle, could push the stern into the lock wall. This tends to squash dinghies, so have someone on the back with a boathook at the ready, just in case you get it wrong.

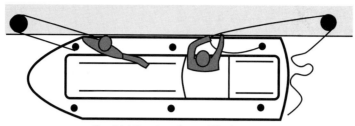

Don't let the stern line trail in the water

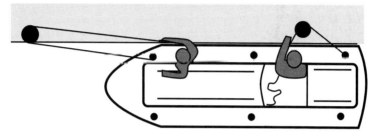

Pull the boat back until you can easily flick the line off

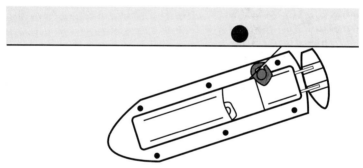

Don't use a lot of throttle when you move off

Fig 10.11 Tips for leaving a lock.

Commercial lock techniques

In the larger commercial waterways, you will often be locked in with commercial vessels. Officially, pleasure boats are never locked in alone, unless they have waited for a period of time and no other vessel has arrived. That period of time varies from place to place, but is usually about 20 minutes. In practice, the policy taken by lock keepers concerning pleasure boats varies from place to place. Except in periods of drought, when it is essential to help conserve water by minimising lock operations, we have never had to wait for other vessels at a lock, except at giant Dutch and German locks, which handle enormous amounts of commercial traffic. Then, it's an altogether different, and very frustrating, story.

Although all locks work on the same fundamental principles, the sheer size of the bigger ones imposes variations on things like water wastage. At Fontinettes – the first large lock that many continental newcomers encounter – if you could drop a terrace of houses inside it, the rooftops would not be visible. That means that, in each lock cycle, a staggering 5 million gallons of water has to be moved! These colossal water movements mean that during descents/ascents in large locks, additional forces are imposed on the vessels inside. The extent of these forces, and how they are dissipated, affects vessels inside the lock, but in the majority of cases the descent will be done at a speed that produces little noticeable effect. On only one occasion (leaving aside those aforementioned giant locks) have we had an uncomfortable lock passage, and that was when we were the last boat to go through a particular Belgian lock before the Easter shutdown. The lock keeper had to do some maintenance after the last boat had passed, so he let the water out far too quickly and gave us a very bumpy descent.

Modern gate sluices

It is common for modern locks to have gate sluices, or for a gate to act as a sluice, as shown in the schematic diagram (Fig 11.1) which represents the operation of the Stadtbredimus lock, on the Moselle. The lifting/lowering gate is in the closed position, with the water level in the lock ready to receive ascending vessels. When the lower gates have been closed, the lock cycle commences.

Electric motors lift the 26 ton upper gate, until it is about 1.20 metres above the cill, thus admitting water to the lock. The water comes in behind a concrete wall, designed to dissipate the energy, so that although the lock takes around 1100 cubic metres of water per minute, there is very little turbulence. Once the water in the lock has reached the upper level, the upper gate is opened, by lowering it down into the cill. When it is fully home, a green light indicates that vessels may leave the lock.

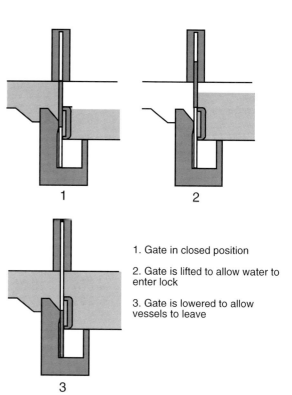

1. Gate in closed position

2. Gate is lifted to allow water to enter lock

3. Gate is lowered to allow vessels to leave

Fig 11.1 Modern gate sluices.

Basic lock rules

If you have a radio listen on the lock's channel. Signs giving this channel may be posted near the lock. Blue and white signs advise vessels of the channel. Red-bordered ones tell them to make contact on that channel. (That obligation does not apply to small craft.) If there is no sign and you don't know the lock channel, first try listening on 18, 20 and 22. If you hear something, listen out for the lock name, to be sure you are listening to conversations about the lock you are approaching, not the one you just passed.

Going strictly by the book, small craft are not entitled to separate locking and must not enter a lock until invited to do so by staff. In practice, it isn't always quite like that. If you are all alone and approaching a large lock in France or Belgium, and you see green lights and open gates, you are, in our experience, expected to proceed towards the entrance. French and Belgian lock keepers rarely give instructions to pleasure craft but will often operate a large lock just for you. Depending on what traffic is approaching from the opposite direction, they may take you up, or down, in the full lock, or just half of it.

At major Dutch and German commercial locks, it is very much a question of playing it by ear. One morning we had 'Yacht, lock full!' bawled at us, over a tannoy, when we tried to follow commercial vessels into a half empty lock. That same day, we were cruising alone and another Dutch keeper used his tannoy to berate us for still hanging back when the lights turned green.

Summary of the lock rules

When you are using locks, in company with commercial traffic, it is particularly important to know the basic rules. Here is a summary:

- If you cannot, or do not wish to, enter the lock, stop before you get to the 'Stop' sign.
- Do not overtake on the approach in, or near locks.
- Enter slowly, to avoid bumping gates, protective devices, or other vessels.
- Where limits are marked on the lock side walls, keep within those limits.
- While the lock is being filled, or emptied, and until you are allowed to leave, use your lines to keep the boat close to the wall and to prevent it from bumping parts of the lock, or other vessels.
- You must use fenders and, if movable, they must be of a floating material.
- Small craft should keep away from other vessels in locks.
- Normally, the use of engines is prohibited from the time a vessel makes fast until it is permitted to leave, but some authorities waive this proviso.
- In locks and lock basins, vessels not displaying a blue light or cone must keep at a minimum lateral distance from those that do. Passenger vessels must not be locked with such vessels. Any vessel displaying two, or three, blue lights or cones will be locked separately.
- Except for small craft, the normal rule at locks is 'first come, first served' but note the following points:

    Fire, police and custom's vessels of countries bordering the river on urgent duty have priority and vessels to which authorities have expressly granted priority (eg passenger vessels on regular service).

    Vessels that are entitled to priority display a red pennant at the bow.

Finally, there is a regulation which says that lock keepers may, in the interest of safe orderly navigation, issue instructions which contradict a basic rule. These instructions should be obeyed. A typical example is, as we mentioned earlier, encouraging you to lie alongside a barge. This contradicts the rule that says you must keep your boat close to the wall and the one which says 'Small craft should keep away from other vessels in locks'.

Approaching a big lock

The techniques for using big locks are different from those we've described for small locks. In many ways it is easier to go through a big lock than a small one, but there are a few traps to avoid, starting with the approach. Once again, get out the binoculars but, if you see anything other than green lights, don't debate whether to moor or not – just do it. For a start, it is often impossible to see the barges in the lock, and when the gates open, you don't want to be in the way of

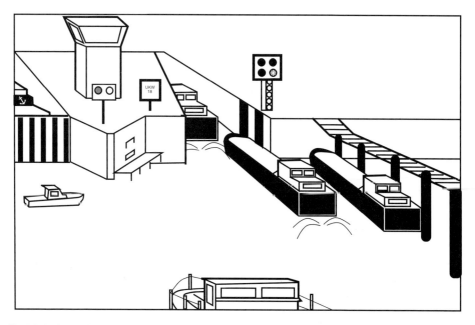

Double locks can be very confusing when viewed from a distance. It is often difficult to read signs and pick out lights, so it is essential to get out the binoculars whilst you are still some way off. Otherwise, like the cruiser on the left, you could find yourself close to a lock that is about to disgorge its contents.

Through the binoculars, you can see that you won't have to go alongside the dreaded piles because a mooring place has been provided for *plaisanciers*. You can also read the sign that tells large vessels that they must contact the lock on channel 18. A black and white light scintillates, adjacent to the next lock to be used, but do not assume that is the one you will go in! You could see half a dozen cycles before it gets to your turn.

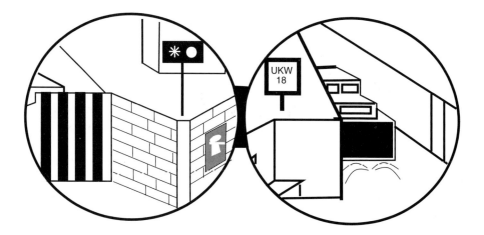

Fig 11.2 Double lock.

many tens of thousands of tons. Secondly, many of these locks have cycles exceeding half an hour, so you could have quite a wait.

Of course, if you have a radio, you can enquire about the state of the lock, but you won't necessarily get a response. French and Wallonian Belgian lock keepers usually respond to enquiries, provided they are in French. In Flemish-speaking Belgium, many lock keepers prefer to respond in English, rather than French. When we have been waiting at large commercial locks in Holland and Germany, we have rarely received a response to radio calls, even though we've always had someone in the crew who had at least a passing acquaintance with both languages.

Mooring before the lock

Pre-lock moorings vary tremendously; at some there are bollards set on a civilised concrete quay, but you will also encounter slippery timber grids and other structures that are less kind to pleasure craft. Most dreaded of all are piles, set at appropriate intervals for barges! Underwater cills are frequently encountered, so those with twin-engined and bilge-keel boats need to be very watchful when coming on to a pre-lock mooring.

The time to leave a pre-lock mooring is when you get green lights, not when you *think* that all the vessels have come out. The cruiser in Fig 11.3 has moored too close to the lock, so cannot see that a fuel barge is at the back of it. (Remember that, in locks, fuel barges must be 10 metres from other vessels.) If the cruiser leaves before getting green lights, he could end up trying to enter the lock just as the fuel barge had reached the gates!

Changing levels

We use three methods for changing levels in deep locks. In order of preference they are: tying alongside a barge, going down on a 'floating' bollard, and leap-frogging down on fixed bollards. As we said earlier, small craft are supposed to keep away from other vessels when in locks, and you would be made to feel decidedly unwelcome if you attempted to snuggle up to a large Rhine ship. However, the attitude of the steersmen of smaller commercial vessels is quite different, and French and Belgian lock keepers have often encouraged us to squeeze alongside a barge.

We wanted to enter Fontinettes on one occasion, but the lock keeper radioed that he couldn't take us, as he would have a full load of barges. At that, a bargee coming up behind us butted in, saying, 'We can squeeze the little boat in'. So everyone nudged up a bit and we were called in and tied, at an angle, between the sterns of two barges. Because of the curvatures of stems and sterns, there was just enough room for two more behind, but I must admit it was a bit alarming to see them looming ever closer!

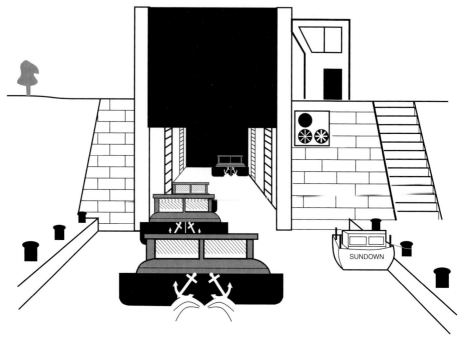

Fig 11.3 Single lock.

If you want to go through alongside a barge and haven't been invited, you should observe the rules outlined in the section about mooring on page 66: get permission and don't stare into living quarters. More often than not, the bargee will take your lines, whilst his wife, on the wheel, will exchange smiles.

Although large lock walls are usually liberally sprinkled with bollards of one sort or another, these are rarely spaced at intervals which suit pleasure boats. Attaching your boat to a pair of inhospitably placed bollards, using the stern line on the first technique, is not difficult. As the water rises, the question is, 'How do you get your lines off the lower bollards and on to the next pair?'

We have read and heard some bizarre suggestions about how to deal with this problem – statements like, 'Just keep motoring back and forth, to change the lines', which not only ignores the fact that engines should not be run in locks, but also the possibility of being between barges. Someone else said, 'Why bother to change lines? Just leave them on and drag them on board at the end.' Apart from the risks to one's own or someone else's propeller, this suggestion conjures up a mental picture of one of the lines jamming!

The way we tackle deep locks avoids any of these antics; we simply put both lines on the same bollard, which is where having a large centre bitt becomes not just desirable, but essential. The other items you need are two short ropes, with loops in one end. Their lengths depend on the size and layout of your boat, so you'll have to decide on that after you have read how they will be used. Drop the

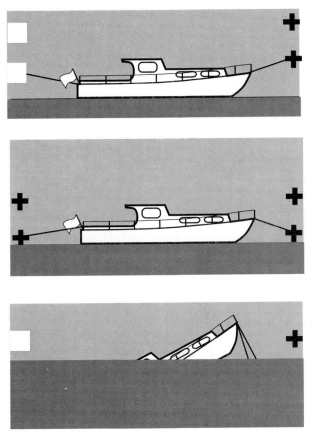

Fig 11.4 Never attach your boat to bollards you cannot easily reach.

loops over the centre and rear bitts. Do not attach them by winding them round the T-bar – you may need it later (see Fig 11.5).

One of the things that makes large locks easier to use is the fact that, because they are so big, you usually have plenty of time for decisions. If you have had some practice and your boat is easily controlled, you will be able to bring it alongside your chosen bollard and stop. The 'rope person' will then be able to deco-rously place both lines over the bollard and hand one of them to the steers-man. If things have not gone quite so smoothly and the lines have been attached whilst the boat still has way on, those free T-bars will help in restoring order.

Once the boat is stationary, it can be repositioned and the lines adjusted so that the vessel lies comfortably against the lock wall. Your aim, if possible, should be to get into a situation where you can tend the lines from inside the cockpit or wheelhouse. Depending on the shape of your boat and the relative positions of bitts and cockpit/wheelhouse, you may want to keep the lines on the stern and centre bitts, or transfer the stern line to the centre.

If you have attached your lines to a 'floating' bollard, you will have nothing more to do until the time comes for you to leave.

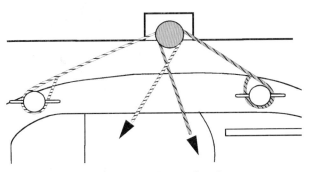

Fig 11.5 Ropes ready to change levels.

Forget about long lines

By 'big lock' standards, the 170 metre-long Stadtbredimus, with its 4 metre level change and 9000 cubic metre water consumption, is something of a baby! Falls in excess of 20 metres are not uncommon, and if you still have any lingering doubts about our advice that you don't need long lines for deep locks, have a look at this imaginary drawing (Fig 11.6) of an 8 metre cruiser in a 170 metre lock with a 25 metre level change. The bollards are set, at convenient distances apart, for use by *péniche,* the smallest cargo vessels likely to use the lock.

To moor the cruiser in the situation shown in Fig 11.6 would require lines totalling around 140 metres! Firstly, with those on board, you wouldn't have room for much else;

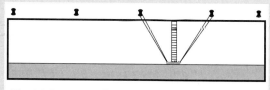

Fig 11.6 Forget about long lines for big locks.

secondly, do you fancy shinning up a slippery 24 metre ladder, dragging that amount of rope?

Of course, there is no need to carry warps like that, nor to do any mountaineering, for, in reality, suitable attachment points would be sited on the lock wall, as well as on the quay. These come in a variety of shapes and types (see Fig 11.7). A common UK type is a simple steel bar, which allows your rope to slide up or down. On the Continent, you are more likely to encounter some form of bollard, set in a recess in the lock wall. In many modern locks, 'floating' bollards are installed. These are mounted on slides, recessed into the lock wall, and rise or fall with changing water levels. This means that ascents and descents through many metres can take place without the need for any adjustments to lines.

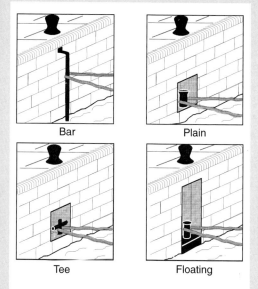

Fig 11.7 Lock bollards.

Leap frogging

However, many older locks do not have convenient bollards, so we've developed a leapfrog technique. For clarity, the following diagrams illustrate 'leap frogging' down using both ropes on the centre bitt, but it's just as easy when the ropes are on stern and centre bitts and when ascending.

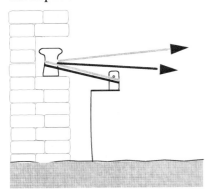

Fig 11.8 Ready to descend using the centre bitt.

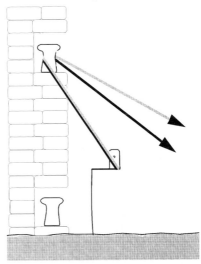

Fig 11.9 Do not be tempted to reach down to drop the rope on to the lower bollard. If the boat rocks, your arm could be crushed! Continue paying out both ropes on the top bollard until the lower one is above the level of your deck.

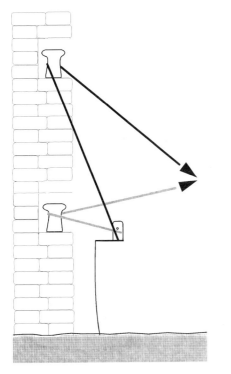

Fig 11.10 When the lower bollard is in a safe position, the person whose rope is uppermost lifts it from the upper bollard and drops it on to the lower one. The other person follows suit and the procedure is repeated until the descent is complete.

REMEMBER! NEVER PUT FIXED LOOPS ON TO BOLLARDS IN LARGE LOCKS. DO NOT TIE ROPES TO THEM, OR TAKE A TURN ROUND THEM. JUST PUT THE ROPE BEHIND THE BOLLARD.

Leaving a commercial lock

When you have squeezed into a lock behind commercial traffic you should always let these vessels get well clear of your boat before you untie your lines – this isn't just because small craft have to give priority to large ones, it's because the combined wash can toss your boat like the proverbial cork. Even when those in front of you have gone, you should still have lines attached if there are vessels to the side of you. The engine of a big barge will produce around 1000 hp and, its prop wash could be damaging to your boat.

Spotting the pleasure boat lock

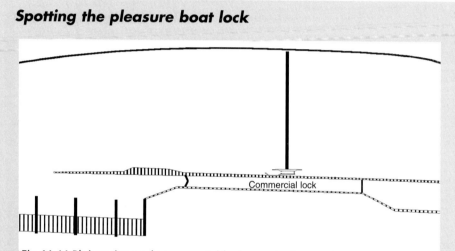

Fig 11.11 Plaisancier *and commercial locks marked on a chart.*

This is typical of the sort of situation you might encounter on a great river, where a pleasure boat lock has been installed alongside the major commercial lock. In case you haven't picked it out, it's just above the word 'Commercial' in the diagram and, as you can imagine, it could be as difficult to spot from the water as it is on paper! Pleasure boat locks alongside commercial locks may be manned or semi-automatic. In the latter operating instructions will be posted. Although the drawing is not to scale, it is a reasonably accurate representation of a lock on the Moselle. The *plaisancier* lock is just a little bit smaller than a 'broad' narrow boat lock, which rather rams home the difference between UK and continental inland waterways.

In some popular Dutch sailing grounds, where huge numbers of pleasure craft go up and down together, *plaisancier* locks can be almost as big as their commercial counterparts. They are often sited well away from the commercial locks and the access route is, usually, clearly marked 'SPORT'. Ample, well maintained waiting pontoons are provided, but these get very crowded in holiday periods.

Canal and river traffic

This chapter describes some of the boat traffic and other river and canal users that you are likely to come across.

Ferries

The number of different types of ferry on inland waterways is legion. On rural French rivers, you sometimes see the 'Attention' sign with the word BAC, which is French for ferry (see Fig 12.1). Often you are still wondering where it is 15 minutes later. The usual answer is that it was so small and infrequently used that you didn't notice it in the bankside undergrowth!

Holland really is ferry land, for in many areas ferries are the only way of avoiding a long road journey. The ferries come in a variety of sizes: some only take foot passengers and bicycles; others carry cars; some are motorised; others run on chains or other devices. The advance warning sign is a white symbolised vessel, on a blue background (see Fig 12.1). If there is a bar under the symbolised vessel, it is a non-motorised ferry. An additional panel may indicate how far ahead the crossing is.

Fig 12.1 Ferry signs.

A ferry sign is another indication that you should reach for the binoculars. Check which type it is, which bit of the river it is on, and whether it is going away from your side or towards it.

All ferries and other vessels operating a regular service, such as water buses, display a green ball during the day and a green light above a white one at night. Ferries on chains, or other fixed devices, display only the green over white lights by night. Those ferries crossing under their own power at night must also have conventional port, starboard and prow lights, unless their contours are made clearly visible by deck

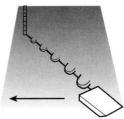

Fig 12.2 Pendulum ferry.

lighting. Strangest of all ferries are the pendulum variety, which swing across the waterway on a chain of linked buoys or small boats (Fig 12.2). The rules for safely passing ferries are: never pass in front of one, and never pass close behind a non-powered ferry (you could hit its chains).

Dredgers

Dredgers are not infrequently encountered in the middle of a canal or river. In most parts of the Continent, they will be displaying red flags on the side they are dredging on, and a red flag above a white one on the other side, to indicate that you must not create wash as you pass. In the UK dredgers normally display a red flag on the dredging side and a white flag on the side you should pass (Fig 12.3).

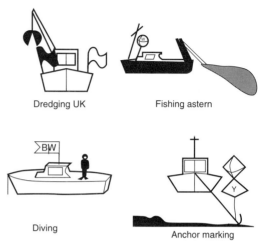

Dredging UK   Fishing astern

Diving   Anchor marking

Fig 12.3 Some flags and symbols.

Fishing and dive boats

If a fishing boat (even pleasure craft) has nets near to the channel, they should be marked by yellow flotation devices by day and white lights at night. However, a professional fishing vessel that is dragging trawls or lines behind displays a white masthead ball (Fig 12.3).

When using other fishing techniques, including side trawling, professional boats display a yellow ball by day and an all-round yellow masthead light at night. You are unlikely to encounter fishing boats other than in estuaries, meers and lakes, but if you do meet a vessel engaged in fishing, don't pass close behind it. Vessels meeting or crossing a boat engaged in fishing or other work that limits manoeuvrability (eg dredging, buoy laying) must give way. When working vessels and fishing boats meet or cross, the working vessels have priority.

A boat being used for diving displays a blue and white panel (Fig 12.3). It is not a flag but a solid metal version of the international flag signal for the letter A. It must be visible from all directions, so two may be shown. If you see the same panel on the bank, diving is taking place in that vicinity. Diving panels are clearly illuminated at night.

Diving for sport is prohibited in areas where navigation might be hindered, particularly on the course of ferries, at harbour entrances or near berthing areas. You must keep a sufficient distance (sometimes specified by the authorities) from vessels being used for diving.

If you see a boat displaying two white flags – one above the other – by day, and the equivalent lights by night, look out for anchor chains. The position of the anchor (or anchors) may also be marked by yellow flotation devices by day and white lights by night (Fig 12.3).

Towing vessels

Vessels that are being towed, by day, display a yellow masthead ball; where there is more than one vessel in each row, both outer vessels display the ball. The towing vessel displays a yellow cylinder with black and white bands at each end (Fig 12.4).

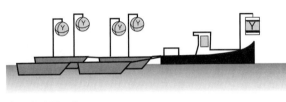

Towed convoys transporting cargoes are not common in Western Europe, but you are quite likely to encounter tugs pulling several lighters, especially where dredging is taking place. Quite often all the

Fig 12.4 Towing.

vessels in the convoy, including the tug, come under the heading 'small craft', and do not, therefore, have to display the signals. We have encountered more than one motley assembly of lighters, with a small tug struggling to control them, and it is best to give these assemblies as wide a berth as possible. It goes without saying that you must never attempt to go between boats in a towed convoy.

Water ski-ing

Water ski-ing and similar activities are only permitted by day and in good visibility. They may be restricted, by the relevant authorities, to a designated area. If you are driving a ski boat, you must be accompanied by a competent person, responsible for the skier; do not trail the tow rope. If you are ski-ing outside an area that is reserved for this purpose, keep a sufficient distance from other vessels, the bank and bathers. This distance may be designated by the relevant authorities.

Bankside fishermen

The attitude of bankside fishermen depends on who got there first. You should slow down when passing, but even then you're likely to get a scowl and we have even had dirty looks when they have had to move off our permanent mooring. On the other hand, when the fishermen have come along after us, they've been friendly enough and these are the occasions to ask if they want to sell some of the catch. They may even offer to give you some.

Official boats

River police boats, fire service boats, customs vessels, and certain other official craft are fitted with the same type of flashing blue light used by police cars and ambulances. If the crew of an official boat wishes to communicate with you, it will either hail you with a loudspeaker or hoist a yellow and blue flag.

Avoiding commercial traffic

Whenever we have asked canal newcomers about their cruising worries, 'Being among commercial traffic' has come a close second to 'Going through locks'. In fact, as we said earlier, you are more likely to have a coming together with another pleasure boat than a collision with a barge. That doesn't mean that either scenario is very likely, for, in thousands of kilometres, we have never witnessed a collision other than the 'Whoops, no real damage done' variety.

Bargees are professionals; they know how to 'drive' their vessels and, apart from holidays and weekends off, they are only interested in getting their cargo from A to B as quickly as possible. The last thing they want is a collision with a small boat and the attendant delays, form filling and questioning that would ensue, to say nothing of the effect on their insurance premiums. They are going to do everything they can to avoid hitting you, even if you have done something stupid and hazarded your boat.

However, as in every other form of transport, accidents do sometimes occur. Earlier, we gave some safety rules which should be standard practice for all inland waterway cruisers. Now it's time to add two more:

- Always keep a good lookout and that means behind as well as ahead.
- Learn the rules, even those which don't apply to small craft.

Two of the most frequently cited causes of collisions between commercial vessels and pleasure craft are: failure to keep a proper lookout and not understanding the intentions of commercial vessels.

Incidentally, on the subject of bargee holidays, never assume that, because a stretch of water is used purely for tourism, you will not meet a large commercial vessel. Bargees like to spend a weekend on non-commercial beautiful waterways, just as much as you do!

Getting along with the professionals

On the whole, bargees are kind to small boats, but attitudes vary from region to region. In France and Belgium, *péniche* owner/drivers exchange friendly waves, catch lines at awkward moorings, and raft you alongside in locks. In Holland and Germany, even bargees on smaller vessels seem less friendly, usually ignoring a waved hand and muttering a grudging Dutch, or German, equivalent of 'I suppose so' when you ask to raft alongside. Those with really large vessels are even more taciturn. It's easy to think they are rude and unhelpful but, to be fair, one must make allowances for the pressures of being in charge of giant vessels with enormous running costs.

There are times when bargees do make life difficult for nearby pleasure craft, but not with malice. A typical example is a technique used for getting a lightly laden barge under a low bridge. The wheelhouse, near the back of the barge, is the highest point, so as the front comes under the bridge, they accelerate hard to raise the bow and dip the back. If you happen to be alongside at the time, you can have a rough ride.

Consideration to owners of commercial vessels is not only something that canal regulations insist on; it is common courtesy. Most barges are the bargee's family home, so mooring against one is a bit like parking your car in someone else's drive! You wouldn't do that without permission, so you shouldn't moor alongside a barge without asking. If you don't speak the bargee's language, try asking in English (a surprising number speak it) and, if that fails, just smile, hold up a rope and point at one of the bollards. Once alongside, ask permission to cross the deck to go ashore, and avoid staring into the living quarters. If the bargee comes out whilst you are sipping your nightcap on deck, offer him a drink. (A Scotch usually goes down well, as it is a change from most bargees' usual tot.) In the ensuing chat you could learn a lot – from the best canalside supermarket in the area, to which routes have problems. On just two occasions, bargees have said 'no' to our request to lie alongside, but each time a reason was given. On one occasion, the barge was due to leave at the crack of dawn; and on the other, the vessel had just unloaded corrosive chemicals and needed to wash down the sides.

Meeting the locals

The inhabitants of canalside towns and villages are usually welcoming, and it isn't only because they see the ever-increasing use of pleasure boats as a valuable addition to other forms of tourism. We pulled in one night, next to a row of houses on the Escaut, and a man came out to point out the snubbers he'd installed. He had absolutely no motive, other than kindness.

Of course, there can be less pleasant experiences. On two consecutive nights in Holland, we were visited by would-be burglars (the only times this has happened to us). We've also heard of people who have been charged to lie at free French moorings. To avoid getting caught in that way, ask for a written payment demand on officially headed, or stamped, paper. If you feel obliged to pay, but think you were cheated, note what the person looks like and report it to the local Town Hall, police or waterway authorities.

Great rivers

Nothing, said or written, can prepare you for that first encounter with a truly great river. We got our baptism at Nimegen. Near the end of the Maas–Waal Canal there is a double lock, and as our gates opened, so did those of the second lock. We headed for the Waal, surrounded by some 100 000 tons of moving steel, and joined the mighty river at one of its busiest and most turbulent points. Our first reaction was astonishment at the sheer volume of traffic, then we asked ourselves, 'Who is "blue boarding" whom?'

We have already mentioned in Chapter 7, that the rules for meeting on rivers differ from those that apply to other stretches of water. Now it's time to learn them.

Blue boarding

When meeting in large rivers, upstream vessels (taking into account local situations and other vessel movements) give way to downstream vessels. However, it is not always possible for an upstream vessel to leave a course for downstream vessels on its port side. A heavily laden vessel may need deep water and the deepest water may be on the left of the channel. An upstream vessel may be struggling against the flow and the slackest water may be on the left side of the channel. Consequently, meetings are conducted under what is colloquially known as 'blue boarding':

- Upstream vessels that are leaving a course for downstream vessels on their port side make no signal.
- During the day, upstream vessels, which are leaving a course for downstream vessels to starboard, display a waved blue flag, a bright scintillating white light, or a light-blue board (with or without bright scintillating white light at its centre) to starboard.
- At night, the board with scintillating light (or a light alone) is used, but we'll keep things simple and refer only to a blue board, for day and night use.
- Downstream vessels acknowledge that they understand that upstream vessels are leaving a course to starboard by also displaying a blue board on their starboard side.

- You can see these signals, whether the boat concerned is in front of you or astern, and they are displayed until passing is complete. They must not be displayed after passing, except when upstream vessels intend to go on leaving a starboard passing course for downstream vessels.

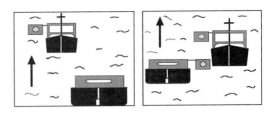

Fig 13.1 Blue boarding.

- If upstream vessels believe that downstream vessels have not understood their intentions about the side they are leaving a course on, they make a sound signal. One short blast indicates a meeting port to port. Two short blasts indicate a meeting starboard to starboard.

Officially, none of the above applies to meetings between small craft and other vessels, or to meetings between two small craft. When two small craft meet, they should, if necessary, alter course to starboard to pass port to port. However, we have been shown a blue board by commercial vessels.

Unofficial signals

Once we were travelling up an unusually deserted stretch of the Rhine. The only boats in sight were us and a large barge, coming downstream. As he drew nearer, the barge put out his blue board, obviously because he wanted to keep to his left and we were hugging the right of the channel. We let him know we had understood, by hanging out a blue towel, and were rewarded by a cheery wave. That was the first time that any steersman of a giant barge had waved to us, so our signal was obviously appreciated. On another occasion, this time near Dordrecht, we were approaching a barge that lay alongside a quay. Again we were the only vessels around and, as he got under way, he showed us a blue board, indicating that he intended to keep to the left bank. These blue board displays were unofficial, a bit like a lorry driver flicking an indicator to say 'You can overtake me', but they illustrate that masters of large vessels expect pleasure boats to be able to understand signals. Other unofficial signals are also used. For example, if you've made an early start and the day is light, but not yet bright, barges will sometimes illuminate a single navigation light. That means 'Have you seen me? Please keep to the side I'm showing this light on'.

Passenger boats and tugs

There are some departures from normal rules for meeting on rivers. Provided that their request can be safely carried out, certain categories of downstream vessels may request upstream vessels to change the course they have left them.

These categories include passenger vessels on regular service, carrying a specified minimum number of passengers (300 on the Rhine), that wish to call at a landing stage on the side used by upstream vessels.

Towed convoys, which are coming downstream but intend to turn upstream, may also request a different course, because their unwieldy nature might necessitate this. However, in any case where an upstream vessel sees that the course requested by a downstream vessel could lead to a collision, the steersman sounds a series of very short blasts and takes avoiding action to prevent collision.

Harbours and tributaries

On the big waterways there are a lot more exits and entrances – canals meeting, harbours, commercial facilities and so on. When you are in an area like this you must be careful not to make a manoeuvre that would force other vessels to have to suddenly change their course or speed.

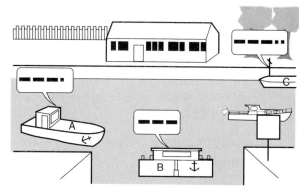

Fig 13.2a *Vessels (other than small craft) that intend to enter or leave tributaries or harbours use sound signals to make their intentions clear to other vessels.*
A *'I want to turn to starboard into the tributary.'*
B *'I want to cross the waterway.'*
C *'I want to turn to port into the tributary.'*

Another important rule is that a downstream vessel that has to turn upstream in order to enter a tributary or harbour must give way to upstream vessels that also wish to enter that tributary or harbour, unless the upstream vessels are small craft. (Downstream small craft must give way to upstream small craft.) When entering or leaving tributaries/harbours, vessels (other than small craft) intending to make a manoeuvre that might oblige other vessels to alter course or speed must give a sound signal. Three long blasts means 'I want to cross the water-

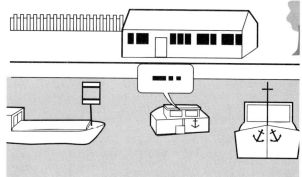

Fig 13.2b *If necessary vessels crossing the channel make a further signal before completing the crossing.*

way'. Three long blasts followed by one short blast means, 'I want to turn to starboard into, or out of, the harbour/tributary'. Three long blasts followed by two short blasts means, 'I want to turn to port into, or out of, the harbour/tributary'.

If necessary, vessels crossing the channel make an additional signal before completing the crossing. One long blast followed by one short blast means, 'I now intend to turn to starboard'. One long blast, followed by two short blasts, means, 'I now intend to turn to port'. Vessels that hear these signals must make any necessary alterations to course and speed.

Exceptions to the normal right-of-way rules

Vessels on main waterways usually have right of way, but in certain circumstances, vessels on a main waterway are expected to change course or direction to let vessels leave a particular tributary or harbour. When this is the case, yellow and black isophase lights flash on the main waterway. Whenever you see those lights, you should exercise extreme caution, especially if you intend to enter the tributary or harbour. Their presence nearly always means that the steersman of a vessel that is leaving a tributary or harbour will not be able to see vessels on the main waterway.

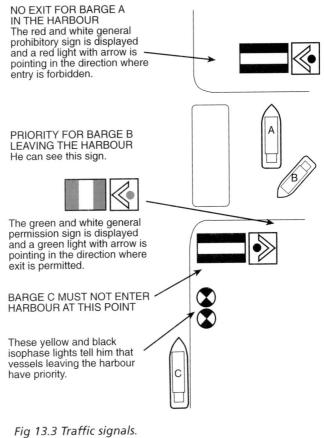

NO EXIT FOR BARGE A IN THE HARBOUR
The red and white general prohibitory sign is displayed and a red light with arrow is pointing in the direction where entry is forbidden.

PRIORITY FOR BARGE B LEAVING THE HARBOUR
He can see this sign.

The green and white general permission sign is displayed and a green light with arrow is pointing in the direction where exit is permitted.

BARGE C MUST NOT ENTER HARBOUR AT THIS POINT

These yellow and black isophase lights tell him that vessels leaving the harbour have priority.

Fig 13.3 Traffic signals.

You may also see an arrow with a red or green light near the entrance to a tributary or harbour or when leaving one. These are often displayed where traffic going into a harbour uses one entrance and traffic coming out of it uses another, in which case they are often accompanied by a general permission or prohibitory sign. Small craft must obey the arrow and light combinations.

Navigating in company

When navigating great rivers you will sometimes feel that you are completely sur-rounded. Don't sail abreast of other vessels if this could cause danger, and never grapple another vessel, nor ride in its wake, without the steersman's permission. When you see vessels displaying cones to indicate that they are carrying dangerous cargoes, keep at least 50 metres from them, except during passing and overtaking. You should not be overly concerned about dangerous cargoes because inland navigation is a very safe form of transport. In 1991, almost 50 million tons of dangerous goods were carried on German waterways, but only 483 cubic metres of hazardous products were emitted into the environment as a result of accidents.

Danger zones

The odds are heavily against you being near an accident involving another boat, let alone one carrying a dangerous cargo, but you should know what to do in those circumstances. On the Rhine and various other navigations, any vessel carrying dangerous materials, on which accident or incident has provoked a release of dangerous materials that the crew cannot control, gives a 'Do not approach' signal. This is the repetition, for 15 consecutive minutes, of one short blast followed by one long blast, accompanied by a synchronised light signal.

If you should hear that signal, you must take every precaution to avoid danger, which above all means putting as much distance as possible between you and the vessel concerned. Other precautions include: closing hatches, portholes etc; stopping smoking; stopping any action which may create sparks; closing down any auxiliary motors (eg a generator) that are not needed.

If you are actually motoring through the danger zone, you may need to turn round and go back the way you came, but, when considering that option, take the effect of the current into consideration. If your boat is berthed in the danger zone, don't hesitate – abandon ship at once.

Read the rules!

Occasionally, we have heard *plaisanciers* complaining about the fact that some countries insist that they carry a copy of the regulations for the canals and rivers they intend to cruise. In fact, *for your own safety*, you should not just carry the appropriate rules, but also have read them, as this extract from the Rhine flood condition regulations illustrates:

Between the Mittlere bridge and Basle, when the water level is between flood marks I and II, all vessels (except small craft without engines) must keep as near as possible to the middle of the river when descending. When going upstream, they should keep in the central third of the river. If local conditions make it impossible to follow such courses, they must slow down and keep as far as possible from banks. Passing and overtaking, within less than 2 boats' breadths of other vessels, is forbidden, and the maximum speed, relative to the bank, must not exceed 20 kph. If the water rises above flood mark II, navigation must cease.

Fig 13.4 shows the 'flood marks' referred to in the extract. You will usually see them painted on walls, either light on dark, or vice versa.

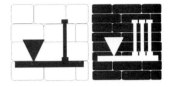

Fig 13.4 Flood marks.

Writing about flood conditions brings us to another topic. Never try to save fuel by allowing your boat to drift with the current. This is expressly forbidden, as well as very dangerous. However, if you find that you are being pushed downstream, whilst facing upstream with your engine running ahead, you will not be considered to be drifting!

Fig 13.5 illustrates something else that might confuse you if you hadn't read the Rhine rules. On certain sections, these warning lights are used to advise upstream vessels about vessels (other than small craft) coming downstream.

A triangle of three luminous white bars means that at least one downstream convoy, over 110m long is in the sector.		Two luminous white bars in the shape of a roof means that at least one downstream convoy, under 110m long is in the sector.	
One sloping luminous white bar means that at least one single downstream vessel is in the sector concerned.		One horizontal luminous white bar means that no downstream vessel is in the sector.	

Fig 13.5 Warning lights displayed on the Rhine.

Tidal waters

For geographic and historic reasons, certain features are more common on Dutch inland waterways than in most other places; these include tides, bridges under which tall-masted vessels can pass, and flood locks.

Everyone expects tides in the Schelde, but many people are surprised when they discover how far inland you can encounter large tidal rises and falls. It is quite a shock, for example, to descend Gouda's Hollandse IJssel lock and find yourself in a narrow channel, surrounded by mud and debris. Good maps and Amsterdam tide tables are essential reading in these waterways!

Because of tidal conditions, and other level fluctuations, height restrictions on many Dutch bridges are marked with yellow and black signs, instead of SIGNI panels. A graduated bar is sited on the bridge to mark the mean clearance and other panels, sited at high and low points of the span, indicate deviation from the mean. You can encounter similar signs – in different colours – in various other places.

On movable bridges, signs marking clearance under the bridge may be used in conjunction with light systems (see Fig 6.12). When red lights indicate that the bridge is closed, yellow lights on the span may permit passage to vessels of reduced height. It is up to you to read the scale etc and decide if you are a 'vessel of reduced height'.

Flooding

Few will have forgotten the horrific floods of 1994, when many Dutch people were threatened with the loss of their homes. Such scenes were extreme, but quite dramatic periodic water level rises are not, so locks may be used to control potential flooding. Three red lights in a triangle are then displayed, sometimes with the words SPUIEN = letting out water, or INLATEN = letting in water. Three horizontal red lights (with or without the appropriate words) means the action is about to happen.

Reduced visibility

Navigating in fog is most definitely something that no *plaisancier* should contemplate. Indeed, in reduced visibility, small craft are expressly forbidden to navigate on rivers like the Rhine, unless they have appropriate radar and a qualified operator. In this case, 'qualified' is not synonymous with 'experienced'. It means the operator must hold a qualification, recognised by the appropriate authority, eg Rhine radar diploma. Nevertheless, there is always the possibility that fog might envelop you without warning, so it is, therefore, essential that you know the regulations and sound signals concerning navigation and mooring/anchoring in reduced visibility.

When under way, vessels must display lights normally used at night and adjust speed to suit conditions, circumstances and the presence of other vehicles. They must stop if they cannot proceed without danger. In deciding whether it is safe to proceed, vessels using radar must take into account that visibility is reduced for other vessels. Vessels under way must post a forward lookout, who can hear or see the steersman. This does not apply to vessels navigating by radar, provided the steersman can hear sound signals.

Unless the waterway authorities have waived this, vessels navigating in reduced visibility must have a radio telephone which can receive and transmit on vessel-to-vessel and vessel-to-shore frequencies. On the Rhine, the radio must be able to keep a listening watch on channel 10, or any other channel designated by the authorities. With a few prescribed exceptions, rules for meeting other vessels do not apply in reduced visibility. Meeting vessels keep as far as possible to the right and pass port to port.

Sound signals when stationary, in reduced visibility

In reduced visibility stationary vessels (including grounded vessels) that are in, or near, the channel and outside a harbour, or designated berthing area, must make a sound signal as soon as they hear a sound signal that indicates that another vessel is approaching.

The stationary vessel will continue to give the signal (at intervals of not more than 1 minute) for as long as the signal of the approaching vessel can be heard.

On the Rhine, by night, the three-peal signal is used in all circumstances.

Class 1 waterways

One peal of a bell, if they are to the left of the channel (for an observer facing downstream).

Two peals of a bell, if they are on the right of the channel (for an observer facing downstream).

Three peals of a bell, if their position is uncertain.

Class 2 waterways

One peal of a bell, whatever their position.

Some authorities may permit the bell peal to be replaced by one long horn blast, between two short ones.

In addition, vessels not parallel to the side of the channel, or positioned in a way that might endanger other vessels, will sound one of those signals, even if they cannot hear a signal from an approaching vessel.

Vessels navigating by radar in reduced visibility

A vessel navigating by radar, in reduced visibility, must take the appropriate action as soon as it sees radar indication of vessels, whose movements or position could constitute a danger, or when approaching sections where there may be vessels not yet visible on the screen.

In all circumstances any vessel perceiving a danger must slow down or, if necessary, stop. On the Rhine, downstream vessels perceiving a danger are expected to take avoiding action by turning upstream if necessary.

Vessels not navigating by radar in reduced visibility

Single vessels under way (including small craft) give a single long blast and convoys give two long blasts, repeated at intervals of not more than 1 minute. Any vessel not navigating by radar that hears that signal, apparently forward of their beam, should reduce speed to the minimum at which they can hold their course and navigate with extreme caution. If necessary, they should stop or turn.

On Class 1 waterways, any vessel not navigating by radar must (on hearing any fog signal) take action to avoid a collision. If it is near to a bank, it should keep close to that bank and, if necessary, stop there until the other vessel has passed. If it is in the channel, especially if it is crossing the channel, it must get clear as quickly as possible. On Class 2 waterways, ferries not navigating by radar give a fog warning signal of one long blast, followed by four short blasts and repeat it at intervals of not less than 1 minute.

Class 1 waterways

Downstream vessels (except small craft) make a tritonal signal, eg DOH ME SOH, which is repeated as often as necessary

Most upstream vessels, hearing that signal, reply by giving one long blast, but convoys give two long blasts.

Upstream vessels give (by radio) category, name, position and direction. Small craft also state the side they are giving way on, others propose a passing side.

On the Rhine, upstream vessels (except small craft) state whether or not they are displacing a blue board.

Downstream vessels reply giving category, name, position and direction. Normal vessels either confirm they will pass on the proposed side, or indicate another.

Small craft state which side they are giving way on.

Class 2 waterways

Downstream and upstream vessels sound one long blast, which is repeated as often as necessary:

They use their radio telephone to give oncoming vessels any information necessary for safe navigation.

Vessels that are equipped with radio telephones must reply and give any necessary information.

Small craft also state their type and say which side they will give way on.

Ferry boats who hear one long blast from another vessel reply by sounding one long blast followed by four short blasts.

They also give their category and their course across the waterway, by radio telephone.

Over to you

As we said at the beginning of this book, variety is the hallmark of inland waterway cruising, so you may well encounter situations that we haven't described. However, if you have read and understood everything we have written here, you should meet the unexpected with equanimity. So, all that remains is to wish you 'Happy Inland Waterway Cruising'.

Getting your boat to Europe and five of its popular ports

Anyone who keeps a boat in the UK is faced with a sea passage when they want to visit inland waterways away from their base. This is no problem if the boat is suitable and the owner competent, but that isn't always the case, and whilst owners can become competent by taking suitable RYA courses and passing exams, boats are more difficult to change.

Taking a trailer boat

If you own a trailer boat, the European canal world is your oyster! Sweden's Dalsland Canal would be at the very top of our list of cruising grounds for trailer boats; it scores pluses for sheer beauty, ease of navigation and lock passages, peace and tranquillity, masses of free moorings and abundant wildlife. (There aren't many canals where you can watch beaver and elk taking an early morning swim!) Norway's Telemark Canal is equally beautiful and, although parts of the shallower lower sections need special navigational vigilance, the vast lakes of the upper part are deep and truly spectacular.

The Scandinavian canals are just a few of many that are easily reached by trailer boat. You could cruise the wider sections of the UK's waterways and go back for the car, either by bus or train, when you needed to skip a 'narrow boat only' section. You could enjoy the plentiful free moorings of Holland's West Overijssel, without having to fight Rhine tributaries to get there. You could drive to Italy, in a fraction of the time it would take to get there by boat, and spend your entire holiday on the Adriatic rivers. You could get a ferry to Brittany, and not waste a single minute of your holiday. You could head for Germany and explore the vast stretches of water around Berlin. Your cruising ground options are inexhaustible and, best of all, if you don't like the area you've picked, you can hitch up and try somewhere else! Tourist offices will supply details of launching sites etc.

At the moment you can't take a trailer boat through the Channel Tunnel, but you can cross by ferry. When checking prices, enquire at the port in the country concerned, as well as at a travel agent or the UK office of the ferry company. You could save enough to pay for a lot of mooring fees. We turned up at Frederikshavn (Denmark) one day and bought a ticket for Göteborg at half the Stena-Ferries brochure price that we had almost booked through the Paris office!

Taking a river boat to sea

If you want to take your river boat (ie one that is classed by the manufacturer or your insurer as 'only suitable for inland waterways and estuaries') to another cruising ground, first find out why it has that classification. It might, for example, be nothing more than the fact that it has rubber window frames and the insurers believe that the windows could pop out if hit by a wave. In this case, they would almost certainly be willing to insure you for using the boat at sea if the windows were covered with boards during the passages. Other boats are only unsuitable for sea passages because they have very small engines, and you may be able to fit a larger version of the same engine without spending a fortune. Of course, the drawback to using your boat at sea could be its hull configuration, eg very little draft, in which case you could ask your insurance company if they would be prepared to give you a policy that covers you for going to sea, on condition that the forecast wind is below a specified strength. If your company says 'no' to that, it may still be possible to get your boat to another area by having it taken there by a qualified passage crew with a professional policy.

The small-ad columns of boating magazines are littered with advertisements from people who are willing to take boats anywhere, but you need to be certain you are getting the right crew. Ask a lot of questions – eg crew qualifications, any 'extras' you might incur – before entrusting your vessel to anyone. Though several deliverers were reticent about quoting, one stated £125 per day + expenses*.

Overland transport is also worth considering. It's a big initial expense, but if you want to use a boat on the Continent you could save in the long run, as you should be able to find a marina mooring at reasonable cost.

Make the sea passage ahead of your holiday

If you are taking your own boat to your chosen inland waterway, we'd suggest that you try to do the sea passage one weekend before your holiday, otherwise you could find yourself weather-bound in Hull when you want to be in Scotland.

There are lots of excellent books to help you plan a coastal hop or Channel crossing, but not much has been written about how to get from the harbour entrance to the start of the canal. This isn't likely to be much of a problem in the UK, where traffic is not heavy and you understand both the set-up and the language, but foreign harbours can be baffling. Even helpful suggestions from port control, such as, 'You can moor near the lifeboat', can cause confusion if you don't know that lifeboats are not always painted orange and dark blue.

The following series of drawings and descriptions of five popular Channel ports should help you find your way about, but remember *they are not to scale* and will help you 'get your bearings' in a colloquial sense, not a navigational one.

*Prices and fees given are based on research done in 1996 and are useful for rough guidelines only.

Calais

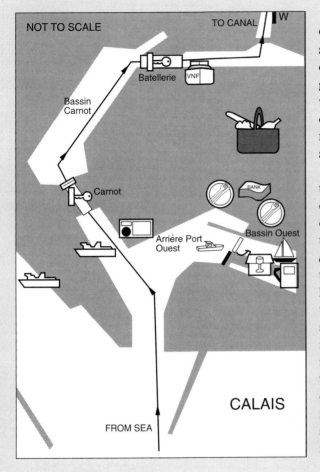

NOT TO SCALE

TO CANAL W

Batellerie VNF

Bassin Carnot

Carnot

Arrière Port Ouest

Bassin Ouest

BANK

CALAIS

FROM SEA

Calais' biggest plus point, as a canal entry port, is its closeness to the UK. Its biggest drawback is the high volume of ferry and hovercraft traffic, which calls for extreme vigilance during approach and entry.

If you have a radio, listen to ferry communications on channel 12; what they say can help you decide what to do. For example, *'Cote d'Azur*, 10 minutes' means that the ferry intends to leave its berth in ten minutes. *'Fiesta*, I'll swing outside' means that the ferry intends to exit the harbour in reverse and turn round when it has reached the open sea. *'Kent*, number 4' means that *Pride of Kent* is approaching the port and is near Calais number 4 buoy.

Showers/toilets for marina users

Showers/toilets for marina users + clubhouse with bar

Showers/toilets for marina users + clubhouse with restaurant

Single cash machine at bank named

Shopping centre

Pontoon

Port control, radio, radar & surveillance

Ferry berths

Marina

Diesel

W Pontoon with water

Lock

Mooring bouys for pleasure craft

Office selling canal permits

Automatic cash machines accepting UK cards

Restaurants

H Oostende harbour office

VNF French canal authority office

Key to drawings.

Calling Calais Port

You too should call Calais Port on channel 12 (English is spoken), when you are near number 4 buoy. Before you call up, decide whether you want to go directly into the canal system, or spend some time in the marina. In the first case, tell Calais Port that you want to enter the *écluse* Carnot (pronounced ehclooze Carno). If the lock is open, you may be directed straight in. If it is closed, you will (almost certainly) be told to 'Pick up a mooring, outside the Bassin Ouest' (pronounced Bassan West). If you do not have a radio, go into the Arrière Port Ouest and pick up a mooring. You can then wait to enter the marina, or go ashore and telephone Calais Port for instructions about entering the canal.

The *écluse* Carnot is open from about 1 hour 30 mins before high water (HW) to 30 mins after HW. During this time, except when the lock is cycling, the gates are nearly always kept open to the tide. At the point where Calais Port tells you to 'Pick up a mooring outside the Bassin Ouest', you will probably be unable to see them. They lie in the Arrière Port Ouest and, paradoxically, because the entrance is wide it is not easy to make out from a distance. Don't worry, all will become clear as you proceed!

Arrière Port

As you turn into the Arrière Port, you will notice a crescent of attractively restored fishermen's cottages on your left. In front of them, on the Quai de la Colonne, there are some very inviting mooring bollards. Do not use them if the tide is receding. The ground under the innermost bollards (ie those not reserved for the small fishing fleet) dries to rock. Don't be tempted by the landing stage, which you will see ahead, near the road bridge that separates you from the Bassin Ouest. This stage virtually sits on the bottom at lowest tide! Several mooring buoys have been provided; those nearest the channel are in the deepest water.

Bassin Ouest

The gates into the Bassin Ouest open at about 2 hours before HW and remain open for about 1 hour 30 mins. However, you can only get in when the bridge is opened, at about 1 hour 30 minutes before HW, and 30 minutes after HW. If you intend to spend a night in Calais, it is better to go into the Bassin Ouest than to stay outside on a mooring buoy, as ferry movements guarantee disturbed sleep.

Mooring

As you enter the Bassin Ouest, you have the choice of mooring on the townside quay (on your left) or at pontoons on the right-hand side, nearest to the clubhouse and office. Electricity and water are not available on the quay, but the moorings are cheaper than the clubhouse side.

The capitaine du port speaks excellent English, as do several other members of staff. Some claim not to, but few seem to encounter problems whilst they are removing masts or supplying information. The charge for craning the mast down (after you have removed stays etc) is reasonable. You may leave the mast on shore, but no responsibility is taken for its safety, so you are recommended to strip it of any fittings. Fuel is available in the basin.

Leaving the Bassin

When you are ready to leave the Bassin Ouest remember that you must depart at the first or second bridge openings (times posted in office window). On the third opening, you will be too late to get through the *écluse* Carnot. Once through Carnot lock, you will be in the Bassin Carnot. If you have not already removed a main or radio mast, this is where you must do so. At the Batellerie lock, at the other end of this basin, there is a fixed bridge with about 4.6 metres clearance. If you can lower your own mast, you may do so alongside the quay that is on your immediate right as you leave the lock. You must not inconvenience any commercial vessels. Masts can only be craned down here by a mobile crane. After the Batellerie lock, you are in the Bassin de la Batellerie and the Voies Navigables de France office lies on the right-hand side, near the bridge. If you need to call there, to get a *vignette* or obtain advice, moor on the left-hand side quay and walk over the bridge. From here you can also walk to supermarkets.

Entering the Canal de Calais

At the moment, bridges on the Canal de Calais are being operated by waterway staff, instead of boatowners, and the operator follows vessels from bridge to bridge. She can be contacted on VHF channel 22, or telephone 21 36 27 98. The operator does not speak any English (which has already caused confusion and problems), but you can get linguistic assistance (during office hours) from Sylvie Bertin of Voies Navigables de France. At the time of writing, plans to take convoys of *plaisanciers* through the bridges, at regular intervals, were being considered.

Calais Port Tel: 03 21 96 31 20
Marina Tel: 03 21 34 55 23. Office hours 8 am to noon, 2 pm to 6 pm.
Voies Navigables de France Tel: 03 21 34 25 58. Office hours 9 am to noon, 2 pm to 5 pm Monday to Friday.
Tourist Information Tel: 03 21 96 62 40. Normal office hours 9 am to 12.30 pm, 2 pm to 6.30 pm, except Sundays. Between 1 July and 15 September, the office is open continuously from 9 am to 10 pm, except Sundays. **Website:** www.pas-de-calais.com/
Emergency services Tel: Police 17, Fire (Pompiers) 18, Ambulance 15.

Gravelines

Gravelines' biggest plus point is the simplicity of the route from sea to canal which is why there is no need for a drawing of the port, but its drawback is that owing to tidal conditions the times when one can pass into the River Aa are limited.

The approach

Gravelines' approach is controlled by Dunkerque on VHF channel 24 or 61. Having entered between the jetties, coming from the sea, you go up the near straight channel to the bridge in front of the Bassin Vauban. The basin has recently been dredged to about 1.1 metres at LW, but there is a cill under the bridge, so access is limited to between 3 hours before and 3 hours after HW, depending on your draft. During July and August and at weekends, the bridge is usually permanently manned. At other times it is opened on request. Telephone the Port Office (English spoken by some of the staff) or call the lock keepers on channel 9. If you cannot enter the basin, lie up on the waiting pontoon. The green and orange lifeboat (marked SNSM) is usually also on that pontoon.

Bassin Vauban

Once in the basin, you will see Flandre Marine's chandlery on the right-hand quay. If you are staying the night, they will direct you to a pontoon. The proprietors do not speak English, but they will, nevertheless, make you very welcome. Diesel is available and masts can be removed by the mobile crane (the cost varies depending on how long the process takes). A small clubhouse serves snacks, or you can walk into Gravelines' delightful centre for a more substantial meal.

Entering the River Aa

Opening times for the écluse Vauban (tel: 03 28 23 19 45, radio channel 9) are 8.30 am to 12.30 pm and 13.30 pm to 17.30 pm. The lock keepers will supply information concerning operation of opening bridges on the river section of the Aa and the lock at Henuin.

Incidentally, we were put off visiting Gravelines for years because of something we read in a pilot, to the effect that it was an ugly, industrial suburb of Dunkerque. I suppose one might get that impression as you approach from the sea, but you will quickly discover that Gravelines is a charming little moated town, which boasts one of France's best preserved Vauban forts.

Gravelines Port Tel: 03 28 23 13 42
Flandre Marine Tel: 03 28 65 34 01
Tourist Information Tel: 03 28 51 94 00. Normal office hours 9 am to noon, 2 pm to 6.30 pm, except Sundays. Sundays 10 am to 12.30 pm, 3 pm to 6 pm.
Emergency services Tel: Police 17, Fire (Pompiers) 18, Ambulance 15.

Dunkerque

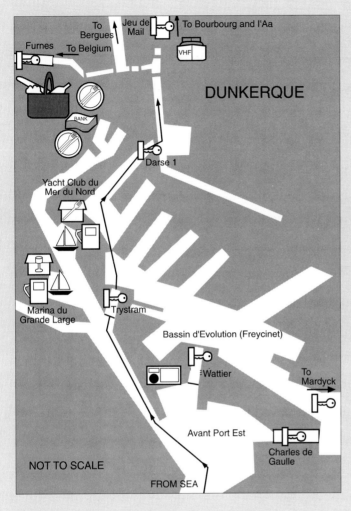

Dunkerque's biggest plus point, as a canal entry port, is the wide range of facilities and interesting places that the town has to offer to boatowners and tourists. If it has a drawback, we have not spotted it.

Port Est

Plaisanciers enter via the Port Est (East Port), far from ferry services and the largest of the commercial vessels using Dunkerque. However, vessels of up to 115 000 tons do enter here. If you have a radio, call Dunkerque Port on channel 73 (English is spoken) when you can clearly see the East jetty. By this time, someone will already be watching you on one of a veritable battery of mainframe-controlled VDUs which provide constant surveillance of the entire port area. If you do not have a radio, the port controllers say that you should go straight into the *écluse* Trystram, if its gates are open for you. If they are closed you should make for the Marina du Grand Large (on the left-hand side of the channel, which is ahead and to the left of you) and telephone from there. Anyone arriving after dark must go to the Marina du Grand Large or Yacht Club de Mer du Nord, as pleasure craft are not permitted to navigate the inner basins at night.

The inner basins

Three locks lead, from the East Port, into the inner basins: *écluses* Charles de

Gaulle, Wattier (pronounced Wot-ee-ay) and Trystram. Once you have gone through any of the locks, there are two possible routes to the canal system, but it is the port controllers, not you, who decide which lock and route you will take. However, you should tell them which canal you are making for as, depending on other traffic movements, this could influence their decision.

De Gaulle is the lock you are least likely to go through as it is enormous and takes about an hour to fill. However, it is possible (but unlikely) that, if a large commercial vessel wishes to enter the Bassin Maritime, you may be invited to join it in de Gaulle. The lock you are most likely to use is Trystram, which has been equipped with ropes for you to hold on to during the cycle. During specific hours, which vary throughout the year and at weekends, Trystram is exclusively reserved for *plaisanciers*. You can get a list of these hours by writing to the Port Authorities. If you arrive outside of those hours, the lock will be opened for you but you may have to wait for commercial traffic. In this case you should moor in the nearby Marina du Grand Large and wait for instructions. There is no suitable place for you to wait near the lock entrance.

Marina du Grand Large

As you approach the Marina du Grand Large, you will see *écluse* Trystram on your right. The clubhouse has showers, toilets etc, and a friendly, but basic, bar. The *capitaine* speaks English. At the moment no meals are available, but a restaurant is planned. At this marina you can buy diesel, get help with mechanical problems, and your mast can be taken down. Mast removal charges vary according to tonnage of the boat. No responsibility is accepted for storing your mast (free), but it will be kept inside a shed. The advantage of this club is its extremely easy access, a definite plus if you have had a roughish crossing and are very tired. The disadvantage is that it is a fair walk to the town; however, bicycles are loaned free of charge.

Yacht Club du Mer du Nord

If you continue past the Grand Large Club, you will see the Yacht Club du Mer du Nord on the opposite side of the channel. The facilities are excellent and the restaurant, which is open every day except Monday, attracts a local non-boating clientèle, which should say all you need to know about the food. The owner and some of the staff speak English. This club is within easy reach of the town and close to various boating facilities, eg marine clothes shop, engineering workshop, sailmaker. Mast removal and diesel available.

Continuing through the system

When you have gone through any of the three outer locks, you will be in the Bassin d'Evolution (shown on some maps as the Bassin Freycinet – pronounced Fray-see-nay). It is almost certain that you will have been instructed to turn left as you leave the lock, but possible that boats making for l'Aa (pronounced la Ah) may be sent to the right.

Having turned left, you proceed past the oblong basins on your right (called by the old word 'darse'). After you have passed under the Mole 2 bridge, there is just one more basin for you to pass, before you turn right into Darse 1. At the end of this basin there is a small automatic lock, whose cycle is triggered when you cross a beam on the approach. If you have any problem, call Dunkerque Port on channel 73. As you leave the lock, under road/railway bridges, bear left on the canal (going right leads to a commercial basin). Very shortly you will see a large bridge in front of you where, immediately beyond it, anyone heading for Belgium, or Bergues, turns off to the left. Vessels making for the Canal de Bourbourg, which leads to l'Aa, should continue straight on and pass through the manned *écluse* Jeu de Mail (pronounced Zhugh de My).

To the River Aa

The approach to Jeu de Mail is a busy area, not simply because of the commercial traffic going to and from Dunkerque port, but because there is a VNF office near the lock. Vessels waiting for cargo instructions from this office lie up on the right, just after you have turned towards Belgium. If you have entered the canal system late in the day and want to spend the night in Dunkerque, you will find a *plaisancier*'s pontoon on the right, shortly after you have passed the waiting barges. This is very conveniently situated. If you cross the bridge, in front of you, it is a short walk to restaurants, cafés and shops. If you have not yet got your *vignette*, you can walk over to the VNF office. A little further on, the Canal du Bergues goes off to the right (no locks). Straight on is the *écluse* Quatre Ponts (pronounced Cat Pont) leading to the Canal du Furnes (marked Veurne on most English and Belgian maps). This lock is semi-automatic (operated by pushing buttons).

The alternative route to l'Aa lies straight ahead if you have gone through *écluse* Charles de Gaulle; to reach it from any of the other locks you have to turn right on exiting, then left near de Gaulle. You will go along the Bassin Maritime parallel to the seashore (beware of large vessels manoeuvring near the commercial quays on your left). At the end of this basin, turn left. The route to the *écluse* Mardyck (pronounced Marr Dike) lies between the land to your left and a mole. The lock is manned; and although the personnel do not speak English, they are very helpful. If you approach open gates only to see them close, this is not a case of someone being awkward. Mardyck is the barrier that prevents sea water getting into the inland waterways and is therefore only cycled using fresh water. Once through the lock you continue straight on, along the Canal Dunkerque–Valenciennes, until it joins the Canal du Bourbourg.

Dunkerque Port Est Tel: 03 28 29 72 62
Port du Grand Large Tel: 03 28 63 23 00
Yacht Club du Mer du Nord Tel: 03 28 66 79 90
Voies Navigables de France Tel: 03 28 25 30 78. Office hours 9 am to noon, 2 pm to 5.30 pm Monday to Friday. Mr Vassem, who speaks English, will sometimes come to the office to supply vignettes, on Saturday morning. However, this is done purely as a favour for English visitors, so do not expect it as a right.
Tourist Information (rue l'amiral Ronarch) Tel: 03 28 26 27 28 or 28 66 79 21 Normal office hours, 9 am to 12.30 pm, 1.30 pm to 6.30 pm Monday to Friday. Saturday 9 am to 6.30 pm. Sunday (out of season) 3.30 pm to 5.30 pm.
Tourist Information (48 digue de Mer) Open during season from 9 am to 7 pm, seven days per week.
Emergency services Tel: Police 17, Fire (Pompiers) 18, Ambulance 15.

Nieuwpoort

Nieuwpoort's biggest plus is that it offers a choice of two easily accessed canal routes. Its one drawback (minor) is that lock keepers may not speak English. The Oostende pilots control the approach and can be contacted on VHF channels 9 or 16.

The Channel to Achter Haven
Shortly after you have entered Nieuwpoort's buoyed channel, you will see a basin on your left. This is still marked on some tourist plans as a yacht club, but for the last 20 years it has been used by the Belgian Armed Forces. Further on, a channel forks to the right and leads to the long-established Royal Nieuwpoort Yacht Club (KYCN). If you want to go straight into the canals, continue along the main chan-nel past the huge marina complex on your left and go under the road bridge into the Achter Haven (rear harbour). Provided you enter the Achter Haven within 3 hours either side of HW, you will usually be able to enter directly into the canal system; call the lock keepers on channel 10 (some English and/or French may be spoken). If you do not have a radio, approach your chosen lock and wait. There are piles to raft against but it may not be necessary as there is ample room to manoeuvre outside the locks. Do not go behind the piles.

Overnight moorings
If you arrive outside those hours, or when hoisted red balls indicate that the locks are being used to drain excess canal water, go into one of the yacht clubs. The marinas on the left of the channel, as you come in, are modern establishments, more reminiscent of certain UK marinas than one's perceived idea of a small Belgian fishing port, but their excellent facilities can scarcely be faulted.

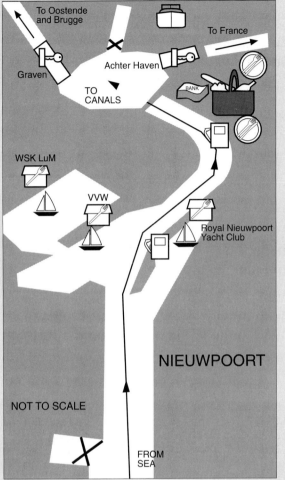

VVW (Vlaamse Vereniging voor Watersport) has almost 1000 places. Moor at the pontoon marked 'Aanmelding' (Just Arrived). Access to shower/toilet/laundry block is by special card, obtainable on payment of a deposit. Mast removal charges apply.

WSKLuM (Waterport Lutchwatch) is in the process of installing a super-sophisticated security system, developed by the club's enthusiastic commandant, Max De Baere, in conjunction with the Belgian Military. Masts can be removed by a mobile crane (organised by the marina).

Both marinas have excellent restaurants. Their drawbacks are 'no diesel' and the long walk or cycle ride that you have to make to get into town. Bikes are available, though.

The Royal Nieuwpoort Yacht Club, on the opposite side of the river, has to be a favourite if you want to visit the town. It also sells diesel and has an excellent restaurant that is much frequented by the non-boating fraternity. Diesel is also available from a fuel barge (*Leigein*) on the right of the channel, as you approach the large bridge before the Achter Haven.

If you have had any communication problems concerning passage through the locks, any of the yacht clubs will help you.

Pilots Tel: 058 29 72 62
Marina VVW Tel: 058 23 69 90 or 058 23 52 32. **Website:** www.vvwnieuwport.be
Marina WSK Tel: 058 23 36 41 or 058 23 34 33. **Website:** www.wsklum.be/visitor.htm
Royal Nieuwpoort Yacht Club Tel: 058 23 44 13. **Website:** www.kycn.be
Lock Office Tel: 058 23 30 15
Tourist Information Tel: 058 22 44 44. **Website:** www.nieuwport.be
Emergency services: Fire, ambulance, police Tel: 100.

Oostende

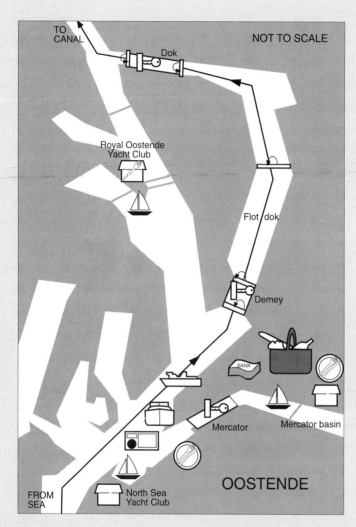

Oostende's plus is that it offers the quickest access to the canal that leads to the popular waterway stopovers of Brugge and Ghent. Its drawback is that you will be entering a busy port (commerce and ferries) after a long and probably tiring Channel crossing. On the approach to the outer docks, call the pilots on channel 9 for details of ferry and commercial traffic, and watch out for traffic lights/arrows that permit or forbid movement in certain directions.

Demey Lock and Flot Dok

If you want to go straight into the canal system, make for the Demey lock. This lock and the turning bridge are operated 24 hours per day and there is a fee for passing through. Beyond Demey is the Flot Dok, which has a turning bridge halfway along and leads to the Dok lock. This lock is nearly always open, but you have to wait for the bridges to be turned for you. *Note*: if you want to spend a night in the Flot Dok, you have to pay an additional fee.

Mercator basin

If you want to spend a night, or moor, in Oostende you have three main possibilities. For a longer stay, the Mercator basin, in the heart of the town, has all the atmosphere you want and the tall ship after which it was named. As you come into Oostende you will have a series of white painted and numbered concrete pillars on your left. If you turn right, between numbers 6 and 7, then immediately left, the channel will lead you to the Mercator sluice. In summer, a waiting pontoon is provided for pleasure boats on the left side. Out of season, if you have to wait for the lock you can moor at the quay, or lie up on a vacant 'trip boat' pontoon. If you need to buy a Belgian canal permit, land here and walk to your left until you reach the Pilot Office (*Loodswezengebouw*).

Mooring fees in the Mercator basin depend on the length of your boat and you should go to the lock office and pay these about 1 hour before you want to leave. Do not go to the lock in your boat unless you have paid; large numbers of vessels go out together in the season, and if one person has not paid everyone is delayed.

North Sea Yacht Club

If you turn right from the main channel, then go left instead of right, you will see moored pleasure boats. These convenient moorings (albeit very close to the fish market!) belong to the North Sea Yacht Club, but we can't tell you anything about them as we have received no reply to our letter and the telephone has not been answered. Maybe you will have better luck in the summer months!

Royal Oostende Yacht Club

Our favourite among the Oostende marinas is the Royal Oostende Yacht Club (KYCO). It scores on atmosphere, restaurant and convenience for the canal route. None of the Oostende marinas have diesel pumps, but if you are in dire need you will find a garage right next to this club.

Masts can be removed in the Flot Dok by a mobile crane. Arrangements can be made via the harbour office, next to the Demey lock. There are no storage facilities. English is widely spoken by lock keepers, other officials and at marinas.

Pilots + obtaining canal permit (Dirk Vanhée) Tel: 059 55 28 11
Royal North Sea Yacht Club Tel: 059 50 59 52
Mercator Marina Tel: 059 32 16 87 or 059 32 16 69
Royal Oostende Yacht Club Tel: 059 32 14 52
Harbour Office Tel: 059 32 16 67 or 059 32 16 87.
Tourist Information Tel: 059 70 11 99
Emergency services: Fire, ambulance, police Tel: 100.

Just going to the Med

To many people, especially sailing folk, France's waterways are just a means of getting to or from the Mediterranean. Whether they enjoy that experience, or consider it a nightmare basically depends on their boat and their preparations.

The intention of this chapter is not to cover the various routes in detail, but to give some sound and very practical advice, starting with the question of whether you should even consider getting there via the waterways.

Planning your route

Whichever route you consider, if you look at the author's map 'France at a Glance' (available from www.boatsyachtsmarinas.com) you will see that somewhere you are going to come across a waterway with a maximum authorised draft of no more than 1.8 metres. It is an offence to enter a waterway knowing that your vessel exceeds the maximum authorised draft, and whilst the French authorities are unlikely to ask you about this beforehand, they would do so if you ran aground and could not get clear. In fact, they would be most likely to unceremoniously dump the boat on dry land, give you the bill and fine you as well. You should also consider the fact that the manufacturer's stated draft for your boat may not be what it actually draws in fresh water, especially when loaded with all the stores etc that you have decided are essential. So, when planning your trip to the Med, there are a number of questions you should ask yourself before deciding on the route.

The obvious way for any sailing vessel to reach the Mediterranean from northern Europe is by sea; down to the Straits of Gibraltar and into the Med that way. There are only two reasons for choosing to get there via an inland waterway: either you want to take a relatively short holiday, cruising only the northern part of the Med; or you don't think you have the experience to tackle the passage to the Straits of Gibraltar.

Taking the second point first, a couple of years back we attended a lunch given for the press after the Catamaran *Club Med* had just won the first 'anything goes' Round The World Race. We shared a table with her navigator and on board weather router Mike Quilter and asked him 'What was the most difficult sea you encountered in this event?' We expected him to talk of the Southern Ocean and

Cape Horn, but to our surprise he said, 'The Med. No sea is so unpredictable.' So if you don't think your experience is up to getting to the Med, it follows that you don't really have the experience to cruise it, unless you are going to spend a good part of your time holed up waiting for guaranteed good weather!

Friends of ours with very little experience bought a boat in the UK and acquired the services of a professional instructor to accompany them to Gibraltar. They regarded this as money well spent, given the tuition they received, and having spent two years in the Med, are presently in New Zealand, after crossing the Atlantic and cruising the Pacific Islands. The moral is that you may start off with ideas of just cruising the Med, on benign days, but could end up needing the skills to cruise the world!

Assuming you are set on getting to the Med via inland waterways, the decision rests on the route to take. Clearly, if you intend to enter the French canal system at a Channel port, you will take the route most suited to your draft. The other alternative, if your draught is less than 1.2 metres, is to go via the Canal Entre Deux Mers but there is a snag; to take this route you have to first defeat the river Garonne and this can be a vicious waterway. It's a good idea to stop at Royan and get local tide tables and advice because we have heard of yachts which didn't have a powerful enough engine trying to dock at a marina on the way and found it impossible! Coming back from the Med can present similar problems. It is not unknown for yachts to take days to cover a few miles going up the Rhone in times of flood.

Once you make the decision to take the inland route to or from the Med, your enjoyment or otherwise will largely depend on how well you have planned in advance.

We mentioned in an earlier chapter the benefits of turning a curvaceous yacht into a more slab sided craft, by using big fenders to the front and rear and smaller ones in the middle, preferably with planks on the outside. Advice on mooring techniques in earlier chapters should also be heeded, but perhaps the biggest problem for a Med bound sailor - draft apart - is that mast!

At locks, you can never be sure which side you will need to tie up on, and a mast splitting a boat in two does not help when quick decisions are required. The ideal solution is to send the mast by road, something that harbourmasters at ports can arrange, but at cost. If you don't want to take this option, then a cradle that mounts the mast in a position that simplifies crossing from one side of the boat to another will be a boon. We have seen people in Calais scrounging wood to knock up a mast support, but advance planning is far better. See page 152 for instructions on how to measure the height of your mast support and other useful information you need to know if making your own.

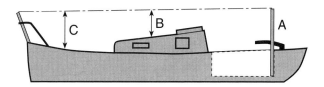

The mast should be mounted in such a position that the tallest crew member can walk under it in the cockpit. You must, of course, check that, with the mast in such a position, you will still have clearance to pass under the lowest bridge on your planned route. This should not be a problem for most yachts.

Clamp a vertical piece of wood to the stern of the yacht, it should be about 20 cms higher than the tallest crew member, Height A.

Clamp a shorter piece of wood to the pushpit; Height C.

Tie a piece of string to the top of each piece of wood, in order to ascertain the best position for a central support and the height of that support; Height B. Check that the tallest crew member can walk under the string at the front of the cockpit. If not, increase height A and re-measure B.

Fig 15.1 Mast support height

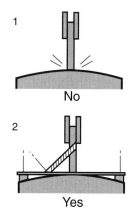

1 The central support will be kept in position by the weight of the mast, so it should not present a localised load.

2 You should give it a wide base and use wooden shims, screwed into the base, to take up any curve. It is a good idea to place a piece of rubber, or strong fabric, between the shims and the coachroof.

The type of support you use at the bow and stern will depend on the shape and type of your boat. You may be able to make a very simple support using just two pieces of wood in the form of a cross.

Fig 15.2 Securing the mast support

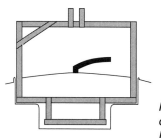

Fig 15.3 Yachts with tiller steering need a more complicated support, like this structure that can be clamped to the rear coaming.

Appendices

APPENDIX

CEVNI/RPNR

Glossary

Assembly of floating material Navigable rafts etc that don't fit any of the other descriptions given here.

Convoy Group of vessels, floating establishments or assemblies of floating material.

  Pushed convoys are rigid groups, pushed by a motorised vessel, behind at least one of the vessels.

  Towed convoys are pulled by one, or more, motorised vessels.

Day Sunrise to sunset.

Ferry Vessels providing transport across a waterway.

Floating equipment Floating machinery for work on waterways, ports etc (cranes, dredgers).

Floating establishment Fixed floating structures, ie boathouses, pontoons.

Night Sunset to sunrise.

Pushed barge Vessel designed, or equipped, to be pushed.

Pusher Motorised vessel designed to push a non-motorised barge.

Shipborne barge Inland waterway vessel that goes to sea on board a vessel.

Side-by-side formations are precisely that, with one of the group providing motive power.

Small craft Vessels under 15 metres hull length (except ferries, boats carrying more than 12 people and pushers), but RPNR include vessels up to 20 metres.

Vessel Sea-going and inland waterway craft (including small craft and ferries), floating equipment.

  Motorised vessel Any of the above, with mechanical means of propulsion.

  Sailing vessel Vessel using sails as only means of propulsion. Vessels that are 'motorsailing' are classed as motorised.

  Stationary vessel Vessel anchored or attached to the shore.

  Vessel engaged in fishing One using nets, lines, trawls or other fishing gear that restricts manoeuvrability.

  Vessel under way Opposite of stationary vessel.

Basic rules See page 60

- Crew must obey the steersman's orders and assist in complying with regulations etc, to ensure safe navigation and good order on board. Do not navigate if your capacity is reduced by intoxication or fatigue.
- Be vigilant, use good navigational practice and avoid endangering human life, obstructing shipping, damaging vessels, banks etc, in or near the waterway.
- *Take any necessary steps to avoid imminent danger, even if that means disobeying these regulations.*
- Your boat's dimensions and speed must be suitable for the waterway you are using and must have enough skilled crew to navigate safely and to ensure the safety of those on board. When under way, the person steering must be suitably qualified and at least 16 years old, unless authorities concerned have imposed other limits. (An engineless dinghy need not be steered by someone over 16.) Crew must be able to hear orders from the wheelhouse; steersmen must be able to hear replies and have a good all-round view, or a lookout to inform about unseen areas. Steersmen must be able to hear sound signals, or place someone to listen out and inform.

Protection of waterways and users

(*Authorities*: the nearest competent authority for the waterway concerned.)
- Don't do anything that could damage waterway installations, eg do not attach lines to signs, buoys etc.
- Don't let potentially damaging objects protrude from your boat. If you accidentally damage, or displace, any installation, or see that this has happened, inform the authorities immediately.
- Do not put anything into the water that could endanger waterway users.
- Do not put petroleum products into a waterway. If you accidentally do this, note where spillage took place and inform the authorities.
- If someone on your boat is in danger, use every possible means to save them. If people on another boat are in danger, or another boat has had an accident that might block the channel, give assistance, without risking your boat.
- If your boat starts to sink or becomes impossible to control, try to get it clear of the channel.
- If you lose something overboard that might obstruct the channel, try to clear that object from the channel. If you can't, inform the authorities.
- If your boat sinks, or goes aground, inform the authorities as soon as possible. Someone must stay on, or near, the boat until authorised to leave. If other vessels might run into yours, send people to warn them. The warning should be given sufficiently far from the accident to permit avoiding action. Display signs to indicate the side with safe passage. (See page 72.)
- If the authorities give special instructions, comply with them. If the authorities want to check that you are complying with regulations, do not obstruct them.

Identifying your boat

Write the registered number, or name, indelibly (eg with non-water soluble paint) on the outside of the boat, in Latin characters, at least 10 centimetres high – dark letters on a light background, or vice versa. If not displaying a registered number, display the owner's name and address in a conspicuous place, either inside or outside the boat. Write the name of the boat, or other identification of the owner, on your dinghy.

Lights and other visual signals on vessels See pages 159-166

Definitions

Height Height above draft marks. If no draft marks, height above hull.

Light Unless otherwise specified, light with a continuous uninterrupted beam.

Light visible from all directions Light projecting an uninterrupted beam through a horizontal arc of 360°.

Masthead light Strong white light projecting an uninterrupted beam, throughout horizontal arc of 225°, and placed to project that beam from the bow to 22° 30' abaft the beam on each side.

Side lights Bright green light, to starboard, and bright red light, to port. Each light projects an uninterrupted beam through a horizontal arc of 112° 30', and placed to project that beam from the bow to 22° 30' abaft the beam, on each side.

Stern light Ordinary or bright white light projecting an uninterrupted beam throughout a horizontal arc of 135°, and placed to project that beam throughout an arc of 67° 30' along each side from the stern.

Boards/flags

Most boards and flags, used as visual signals on board vessels, are rectangular. Colours must not be faded or dirty. Smallest dimension should be at least 1 metre (on small craft, it may be 60 centimetres).

Cylinders, balls, cones and bicones

These may be replaced by items having the same appearance from a distance. Colours must not be faded or dirty. Cylinders should be at least 80 centimetres high and 50 centimetres in diameter. Balls should be at least 60 centimetres in diameter. Cones should be at least 60 centimetres high with base diameter of at least 60 centimetres. Bicones should be at least 80 centimetres high with base diameter of at least 50 centimetres.

Prohibited markings

Do not use lights/signals, except those described in the regulations. (You can use others to signal to another vessel or the shore, provided they are unlikely to be confused with those in CEVNI/RPNR.) Do not use lamps or searchlights in a manner that might dazzle, endanger or inconvenience navigation.

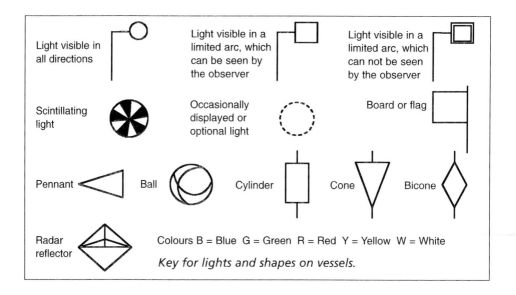

Light visible in all directions

Light visible in a limited arc, which can be seen by the observer

Light visible in a limited arc, which can not be seen by the observer

Scintillating light

Occasionally displayed or optional light

Board or flag

Pennant

Ball

Cylinder

Cone

Bicone

Radar reflector

Colours B = Blue G = Green R = Red Y = Yellow W = White

Key for lights and shapes on vessels.

Emergency lighting

If a bulb fails, you may temporarily replace it by one of the next lowest intensity.

Sound signals See page 70.

Definitions

Short blasts – about 1 second.

Long blasts – about 4 seconds.

Interval between – about 1 second.

Series of very short blasts – at least six blasts of about G second, separated by G second pauses.

Three-tone signal – three different blasts (no pause between). Series starts with lowest note and difference in blasts is at least two notes, eg DOH ME SOH.

Bell peal should last about 4 seconds. Alternative is one metal object repeatedly striking another over 4 seconds.

On the Continent, do not use sound signals other than those mentioned in CEVNI/RPNR. Do not use those signals in circumstances other than those pre-scribed. You may use other signals to communicate with another vessel, or shore station, provided they cannot be confused with any in these regulations.

General sound signals See page 70.

LIGHTS AND SHAPES

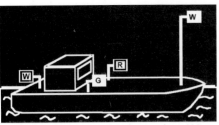

Single motorised vessel no longer than 110 m

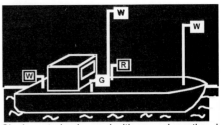

Single motorised vessel with second masthead light – compulsory on vessels longer than 110 m

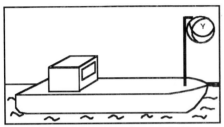

Motorised vessel temporarily preceded by an auxiliary motorised vessel

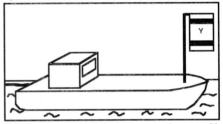

Motorised vessel leading a convoy alone or with other vessels

Motorised vessel leading a convoy alone

One of several motorised vessels leading a convoy

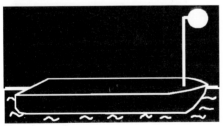

Towed vessel

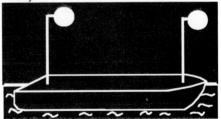

Section of a convoy more than 110 m long

If vessels are being towed side by side, only the outer vessels display the balls or lights. By night, the last vessel (or outer vessels) in a towed convoy shows white stern lights.

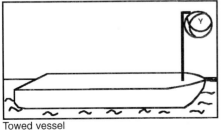

Towed vessel

Fig A.1

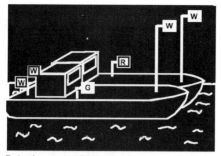

Pair of motorised vessels

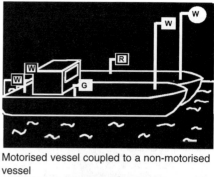

Motorised vessel coupled to a non-motorised vessel

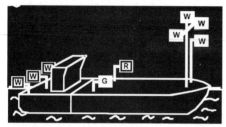

Pushed convoy

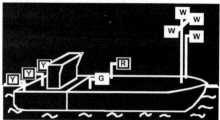

Pusher preceded by one, or more, motorised vessels – eg under tow

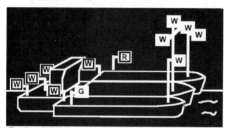

Pusher with barges protruding at each side

Sailing vessel

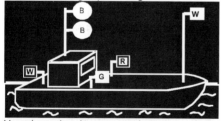
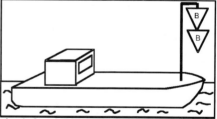

Vessel carrying dangerous substances – there may be 1, 2 or 3 cones or lights

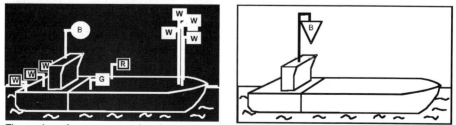

The pusher of a convoy carrying dangerous substances displays these symbols

Fig A.1 continued

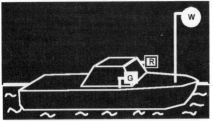

Small motorised craft

Small motorised craft

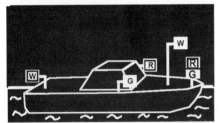

Small motorised craft

Small motorised craft under 7 m long

Small craft sailing

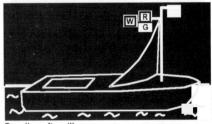

Small craft sailing

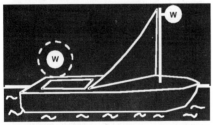

Small craft (under 7 m) sailing – second light
shown on approach of other vessels

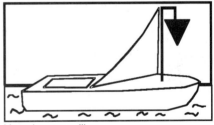

Vessel motor sailing

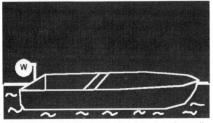

Small craft neither motorised nor under sail

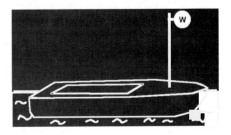

Fig A.1 continued

Ferry not having priority moving independently

Ferry moving independently and having priority

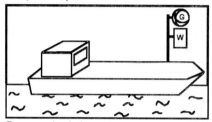

Ferry moving independently and having priority

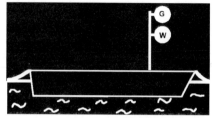

Ferry not moving independently

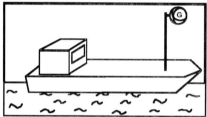

Ferry not having priority, whether moving independently or not

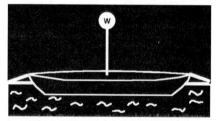

Lead boat, or float, of pendulum ferry

Additional markings for official vessels en route. Blue scintillating = police, fire service, other officials. Yellow scintillating = waterway work vessels

Vessel under 20 m long, authorised to carry more than 12 passengers

Vessel having priority

Fig A.1 continued

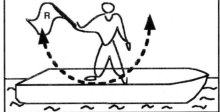

Vessel unable to manoeuvre – small craft may use a white light at night

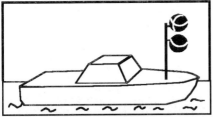
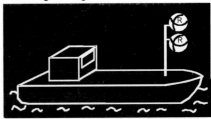

Vessel unable to manoeuvre

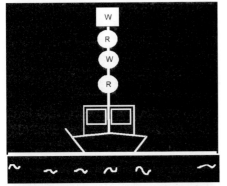

Markings which may be displayed by vessels whose ability to manoeuvre is limited

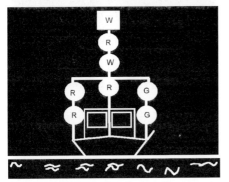

Markings which may be displayed by vessels whose ability to manoeuvre is limited and which are causing an obstruction. Green lights or black bicones mark the clear side

Fig A.1 continued

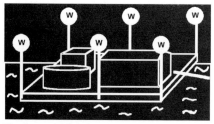

Floating establishment or assembly of material underway

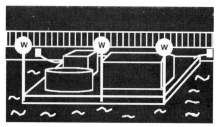

Floating establishment or assembly of material made fast to the bank

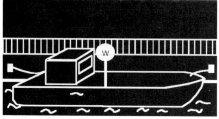

Vessel made fast to the bank

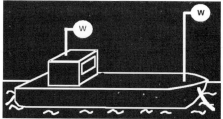

Vessel stationary offshore

Vessel stationary offshore

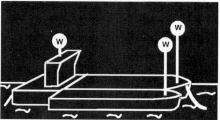

Convoy stationary offshore

Notes

• A vessel is considered to be made fast to the bank even if it is indirectly attached to the bank, eg rafted alongside another vessel.

• When a pushed convoy is stationary offshore, all vessels in the convoy display the markings.

• When a pusher leaves its convoy, at night, an additional all round white light is displayed on the stern of one of the vessels in the convoy.

• Vessels stationary offshore, which are carrying dangerous cargoes, display the blue cones or lights which they display when underway.

• Small craft display the same markings as normal vessels, when stationary offshore.

• At night, ferry boats which are made fast to their landing stage display the markings which they display when underway.

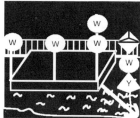

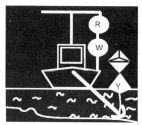

Vessels, floating establishments etc whose anchors might be a danger to navigation display additional markings. Red over white light is displayed when a vessel also needs protection from wash.

Fig A.1 continued

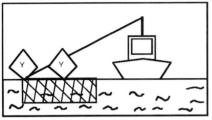

Additional markings for stationary vessels using nets or poles

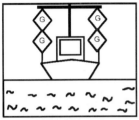 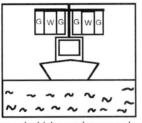 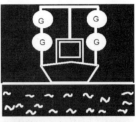

Additional markings for a working vessel which may be passed on either side

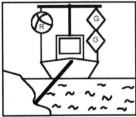 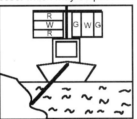 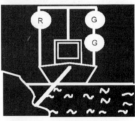

Additional markings for a working vessel which may not be passed on the side where red is

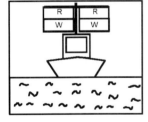

Working vessel which may be passed on either side but must be protected from wash

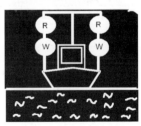

Working vessel, or vessel which has sunk or gone aground, which may only be passed on the side where red and white flags, or lights, are shown and must be protected from wash

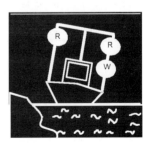

Fig A.1 continued

Fishing

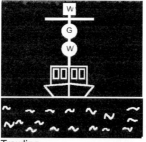

Trawling

Fishing other than trawling

Fishing, other than trawling, with tackle more than 150 m to the-side of the vessel

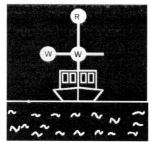

Vessel being used for diving

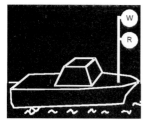

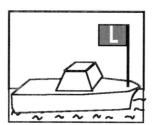

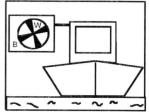

Additional markings for pilot vessels

Starboard to starboard meeting

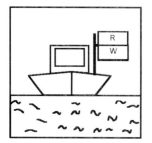

Vessel needs to be protected against wash

Vessel engaged in mine sweeping. You must not approach within 1000 m

Fig A.1 continued

A red light, flag or any other suitable red object, waved in a circle, or repeated slow up-and-down arm movements

Red parachute flare or rocket, throwing out red stars. Flames and smoke from burning oily waste. Red flag with a ball, or something resembling a ball

SOS flashed in Morse code or repeated sounds such as long horn blasts, bell peals or whistles

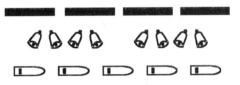

Fig A.2 Distress signals.

Boarding
prohibited

Smoking
prohibited

No berthing within 10 lateral metres of the vessel

Fig A.3 Signs on vessels.

BERTHING FOR VESSELS CARRYING DANGEROUS CARGOS

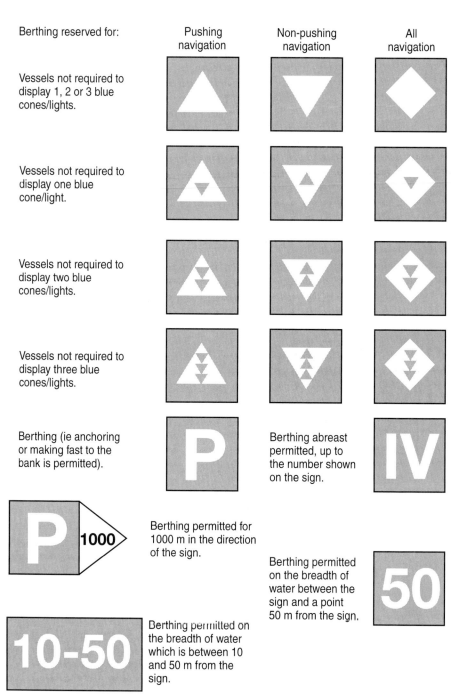

Fig A.4

Rules of the Road

Definitions

Upstream On rivers, vessels travelling upstream are going towards the source. On canals, vessels ascending locks are usually considered to be travelling upstream but, on some canals, the authorities may use other definitions.

Upstream vessel One travelling upstream.

Downstream vessel One travelling downstream.

Meeting Two vessels approaching in opposite, or nearly opposite, directions.

Overtaking One vessel (overtaking vessel) coming to 22.5° abaft the beam of another vessel (overtaken vessel) then passing it.

Crossing Two vessels approaching in circumstances other than 'overtaking' or 'meeting'.

Waterway classification

Class 1 Normally comprises rivers. *Class 2* Canals, lakes and broad expanses.

(**Note**: **1** *The definition of Class 1 and 2 waterways in CEVNI is not the same as the definition of waterway classes according to carrying capacity.* **2** *Authorities may classify waterways differently from above.*)

General principles

High-speed vessels (eg hydrofoils/hovercraft) must not interfere with the course, or manoeuvres, of others.

When Rules of the Road do not apply to small craft in relation to others, small craft steersmen must give other vessels room to hold courses and manoeuvre. Small craft may not require other vessels to give way.

Crossing rules See page 91-2.

No vessel, proceeding with no danger of collision, shall make a course, or speed, alteration that gives rise to a possible danger of collision.

Normally, when a vessel meets, or crosses, a small craft, it maintains course and speed, but if the vessel finds itself in a position where the small craft is in danger, it should manoeuvre to avoid collision. However, RPNR (and some other rules) do not require commercial vessels to change speed, or course, to avoid collision with small craft. Vessels are, however, bound by the general obligation not to endanger another vessel or person on board.

Priority during meeting and crossing See pages 91.

If your small craft has priority over another small craft, but you realise that your position/actions could put that craft in danger, manoeuvre in the manner most likely to ensure that collision (with the small craft concerned, or any other vessel) does not occur.

Normal rules for meeting
Class 1 waterways. See page 128. Class 2 waterways. See page 72.

Departure from normal rules for meeting
Class 1 waterways. See page 131.

Class 2 waterways. Vessels may, in exceptional circumstances (and if safe to do so), request to pass starboard to starboard. (Waterway authorities may define 'exceptional circumstances', eg when a cross-wind prevents a light vessel keeping to the right.) In such cases, vessels sound two short blasts and, if required to do so, display a blue board.

A vessel being met cedes to the request by sounding two short blasts and, if necessary, altering to leave sufficient room to starboard. If required to do so, vessels also display blue boards. If the vessel met sees that the course requested by a downstream vessel could lead to a collision, it sounds a series of very short blasts and the steersman takes avoiding action.

Meeting in narrow channels See page 75.
If small craft under sail and small craft of another category are likely to meet in a narrow channel, sailing boats proceed and other craft await their passing.

If sailing boats are likely to meet in a narrow channel, windward craft have priority. If both are going with the wind, craft with wind to starboard have priority. (See also page 91.)

Meetings prohibited by signs See page 76.

Overtaking
Definitions: *Overtaking vessel* Vessel overtaking, or intending to overtake, another. *Overtaken vessel* Vessel being overtaken, or about to be overtaken.

Except when being overtaken by a small craft, the overtaken vessel will, if necessary, slow down and take any other steps to enable the manoeuvre to be carried out quickly and safely.

Normally, the overtaking vessel passes down the port side of the overtaken vessel, but if the channel is sufficiently wide, it may pass down the starboard side.

Signals during overtaking
2 long + 2 short blasts (from the overtaking vessel) = 'I want to overtake to port'.
2 long + 1 short blast (from the overtaking vessel) = 'I want to overtake to starboard'.
1 short blast (from the overtaken vessel) = 'You can overtake to port'.
2 short blasts (from the overtaken vessel) = 'You can overtake to starboard'.
5 short blasts (from the overtaken vessel) = 'You cannot overtake'.

Signs prohibiting overtaking See page 76.

Prescribed courses See page 68.

Turning See page 80.
If a turning manoeuvre will mean that other vessels will have to make any course or speed alteration, any vessel wanting to turn must announce its intention, in good time, by a sound signal. On hearing a signal, other vessels must (as far as it is necessary and possible) make any alterations in course and speed to enable the turn to be made safely. In particular, if a vessel needs to turn into the current, other vessels must do their utmost to assist.

Signs concerning turning See page 80.

Leaving a berth
Rules for leaving a berth are as those for turning, except that sound signals are one short blast when vessels are approaching to starboard and two short blasts when vessels are approaching to port. This rule does not apply to ferries.

Prohibition of entering a space between vessels in a towed convoy See page 125.

Crossing waterways, entering tributaries, entering and leaving harbours See pages 130 and 131.

Sailing near other vessels See page 134.

Aquatic sports See page 125.

Trailing anchors etc See page 68.

Drifting See page 135.

Wash See page 85.

Signs and signals prohibiting making wash See pages 72 and 85.

Suspension of navigation See page 68.

Passing working equipment and sunken vessels See page 72.

Ferries
Ferries must only cross waterways when other vessel movements make it safe to do so. They must not force other vessels to suddenly change course or speed. Ferry boats not moving independently must not remain in the channel longer

than necessary. When not operating, they must lie at a designated berth, or outside the channel. If a longitudinal ferry cable may block the channel, the ferry must not stop on the side opposite the fixation point longer than is strictly necessary to embark and disembark passengers. Vessels approaching during embarking, or disembarking, may request that the channel is cleared, by sounding one long blast in good time.

Passage under bridges and through weirs See page 66.

Passing under movable bridges
When passing under movable bridges, steersmen must obey instructions given by bridge staff. On approaching, vessels must reduce speed and must not overtake unless instructed to do so by bridge staff. If they cannot, or do not wish to, pass through the bridge and the 'stop' sign is displayed, they must stop before it.

Signals regulating passage under movable bridges See page 68.

Passage through weirs See page 66.

Passage through locks See page 114.

Entering and leaving locks See pages 68, 115, and 122.

Priority of passage at locks See page 115.

Special rules

Priorities of working and fishing vessels See page 124.

Minesweeping
Vessels must not approach within 1000 metres of a vessel engaged in minesweeping.

Water ski-ing etc See page 125.

Fishing
Trolling with vessels abreast is only permissible by special decree. (Passing fishing boats (see page 124).)

Diving for sport See page 124.

Berthing See page 69.

Berthing in the vicinity of certain vessels
(Vehicles displaying cones (see page 35).) There are different rules for vessels bearing cones or lights moored near other vessels carrying cones or lights.

Watch and surveillance

An efficient watch must be maintained on a vessel lying in the channel. Other berthed vessels must be under surveillance by a competent person, who can act quickly if the need arises.

Navigation in reduced visibility See page 134.

Supplementary RPNR (Rhine rules)

Do not approach p 134

Basic

Only small craft may overtake between the Mittlere Rhein and Dreirosen bridges, where upstream vessels must make at least 4 kph, relative to the bank. Before approaching the port basin, downstream vessels should turn in the river and only make for the entrance when it is clearly visible and they are in line with the current.

Grand Canal d'Alsace and canalised Rhine

Normal meeting rules do not apply. Vessels must pass port to port, except close to locks where they may request starboard to starboard passing. Barrages, motive power and factory discharge canals are marked with no entry signs. DO NOT PASS. Stopping, or berthing is prohibited, except at lock waiting points and over-flow canals (downstream of locks).

Ferry from Seltz to Plitterdorf

Passage across the ferry course is carried out under rules for passing movable bridges.

Between mouth of Neckar and Lorch and between Duisberg and the German/Dutch border

Normal meeting rules do not apply. Except for certain circumstances (eg entering a tributary) which would be facilitated by a starboard to starboard meeting, vessels must pass port to port.

Old Rhine

Navigation is authorised on various sections. At Lampertheim, speed limit is 5 kph relative to bank. At Stockstadt – Ehrfelden and at Ginsheim, speed limit is 12 kph relative to bank.

Between Lorch and St Goat

Except for small craft, upstream vessels follow the left bank and downstream vessels follow the right bank.

Mouth of the Moselle
Except for small craft, upstream vessels (not intending to enter the Moselle) must be 80 m (minimum) from the bank. Before entering ports between Duisbourg and Ruhrort downstream vessels (other than small craft) must turn in the river and only approach when they can see the entrance and are in line with the current. Sailing is forbidden between pk 777.5 and pk 785.5.

Night navigation between Bingen and St Goar
Vessels must use a radio telephone on channel 10. Downstream vessels must also use radar.

German army boats
German army boats (between Iffezheim locks and Spijk ferry) display a scintillating yellow mast light by day and night.

Navigating in reduced visibility downstream of Spijk ferry
Vessels must keep right. Downstream vessels using radar sound 1 long note (not Doh/Me/Soh).

Flood restrictions.
Mittlere bridge to Basle. See page 134.

Between Kembs locks and Iffezheim locks.
Locks cease to operate when flood mark II on the wall below the lock is reached.

At Strasbourg
Red lights before north and south ports warn vessels that navigation is suspended.

Warning signals See page 135.

Rhine roadsteads and refuge ports
Roadsteads are marked by the letter 'R' below a red bordered white square. An additional triangular panel may indicate the length for which the roads extend. Other panels may indicate types of boat which may wait. Refuge ports may only be used for specified periods.

Waste disposal
Bilge water must be collected in containers and stored in a manner which eliminates any possibility of spillage into the river. Waste oil/oily mixtures must not be kept on deck. Household rubbish and slops must not be thrown into the river. Waste oil, bilge water and household rubbish can be disposed of at designated areas.

APPENDIX

Useful addresses

www.boatsyachtsmarinas.com/France
Web site edited by Marian Martin, devoted to cruising inland France, with information on hire boat towns, trailer boat towns, waterways, boats, books & cruising tips.

Boat hire

Ad Navis
www.adnavis.com
Boat hire in Germany, France, Holland & Finland

Alvechurch Boat Centres
www.alvechurch.com
Canal boat holidays in England and Wales. Canal narrowboats up to 5-key quality. Four bases on the UK canal network.

Association of Pleasure Craft Operators (APCO)
email: apco@britishmarine.co.uk
Information on UK narrowboat and cruiser hire; hotelboats etc in all areas and from several companies.

Barge Connection
www.bargeconnection.com
A US based agency representing hotel barges and self-drive vessels on the inland waterways of France, Holland and the UK.

Barging in France
www.barginginfrance.com/index.htm
An agency based in Saint-Jean-de-Losne, France, offering fully catered and self-operated houseboat and barge holidays in France, Germany, Holland and Ireland.

Blakes Boating Holidays
www.blakes.co.uk
Offering a choice of boating holiday destinations - from Scotland to Florida; Holland to the Norfolk Broads.

Burgundy Cruisers
www.bourgogne-fluviale.com
Boat hire throughout France, run by English people.

Canal Barge Holidays
www.canalbargeholidays.com
International booking specialists in the field of canal boat holidays throughout the world.

Connoiseur and Emerald Star
www.connoisseurafloat.com
French, Irish, English, Belgian,
German & Italian inland waterway
holidays.

Crown Blue Line
www.crownblueline.com
Offering rental boats on the inland
waterways of Europe with 22
departure bases in some of the most
beautiful regions of France, Germany,
Holland, Ireland, Italy and Scotland.

Dalsland Turistrad Sweden
www.dalsland.com/eng/
Boat hire; general tourist information;
canal maps and handbooks (in
English if requested).

Europe Afloat
www.canalboat.org
All inland boat hirers of Europe listed
per country and region. Hand-picked
links to quality background information.

Friesland Boating
www.friesland-boating.nl
Boat hire in Holland, Germany &
Ireland; also skippered charter on
larger vessels.

Hoseasons Holidays
www.hoseasons.co.uk
Holidays throughout Britain, France,
Belgium, Italy and Germany including
self-drive boating holidays.

Locaboat Holidays
www.locaboat.com/index_an.html
Offering a broad range of pénichette
canal cruisers for hire in France,
Germany, Holland and Ireland.

Maine Anjou Rivères
www.maine-anjou-rivieres.com
Agency offering river and canal cruising throughout France.

Nautic
www.nautic.fr
Booking agent for canal boat rentals
in the south of France.

Navtours
www.navtours.com
Offering bareboat charters, crewed
charters and sailing instruction on
the waterways of Ireland, France,
Holland and Germany.

Nicols
www.nicols.com/ang1.html
Self drive boats for hire on the rivers
and canals of France and northern
Germany.

Viking Afloat
www.viking-afloat.com/
Self-drive boating holidays in superb
boats on the canals, rivers and inland
waterways of England and Wales.

Waterweb Fluvial
www.fluvial.artourisme.com/
welcome.asp
Multi-lingual booking site to busi-
nesses that offer self-drive motor
cruisers and hotel barges in Southern
France.

Waterway Holidays
www.waterwaysholidays.com
Self-drive boating holidays on UK
canals and waterways with instant
online boat availability.

Authorities and organisations

ANWB
www.anwb.nl
Dutch maps, almanacs with regulations, marina details etc and tourist information.

British Waterways
www.british-waterways.org
UK regulations; permits; UK maps; canal cruising videos.

Comité de Surveillance
Service de la Navigation
37 rue du Plat
59304 Lille Cedex
France
Tel: +33 3 20 15 49 70
Can arrange French competence tests for UK citizens.

Dienst voor de Scheepvaart
Havenstraat 44
3500 Hasselt, Belgium
Belgian regulations, canal permits; general tourists information.

HISWA
www.hiswa.nl/marketplace/quick-search.asp?maincat=11400
Click on Diverse makelaars or Hiswa makelaar for information on Dutch yacht brokers (Makelaar)

NUMIJ
www.numij.nl
Dutch and Rhine regulations in Dutch.

RYA
www.rya.org.uk
Training courses and information.

Saimaa Canal
www.lappeenranta.fi/satama/english/contacts.htm
Regulations; permit charges etc for Saimaa Canal; tourist information.

Ships Radio Licensing
www.radiolicencecentre.co.uk/rlc/
For operators certification see
www.rya.org.uk

Voies Navigables de France
www.vnf.fr.
French canal permits; general French maps, tourist information.

Tourist information, book and map suppliers

www.boatsyachtsmarinas.com/ France
Web site edited by Marian Martin, devoted to cruising inland France, with information on hire boat towns, trailer boat towns, waterways, boats, books & cruising tips.

Binnenshiffahrt Verlag Gmbh Haus Rhein
Dammstr 15-17
D47119 Duisberg, Germany
Books and maps of German and Dutch waterways and regulations (German).

Conseil Régional Nord-Pas de Calais
BP 2035
59014 Lille Cedex
France
Maps of Flanders/Northern France; general tourist information.

Inland Waterways Association
www.waterways.org.uk
Charity looking after the interests of waterway users and suppliers of charts and books.

Kelvin Hughes Ltd (Southampton)
www.bookharbour.com
Charts/maps of estuary and coastal waters; books.

Navicarte
www.guide-fluvial.com
Belgian and French maps.

Nicholson
77-85 Fulham Palace Road
London W6 8JB
England
Publishers of the Nicholson Ordinance Survey guides to the inland waterways of the UK.

Telemarkreiser
www.telemarkreiser.no/
Details of local hire firms; tourist information in Norway.

Westtoer apb
Koning Albert I-laan 120
B-8200 Sint-Andries
Belgium
E-mail: info@westtoer.be
Tourist Navigation Guide. For western Belgium (West and East Flanders, Hainaut, Brabant and Brussels and Region Nord-pas de Calais. Supplied in Dutch/French and English/German).

Index